FALLEN AMONG SCRIBES

Conversations With Novelists, Poets, Critics

DAVID GERARD

For David, who would probably have
preferred more playwrights inside
these pages

——— good wishes,
David Gerard

FALLEN AMONG SCRIBES

Conversations With Novelists, Poets, Critics

DAVID GERARD

ELVET PRESS
1998

© David Gerard and the contributors

First published in 1998
by Elvet Press in Great Britain,
9 Crofters Green, Wilmslow, Cheshire SK9 6AY

Typeset in 10½pt Berkeley Old Style by Printdesigns Wilmslow

ISBN 0 9510776 8 6

Fore-word

Writers reflecting on their work are of perpetual interest to readers: we hope to gain some insight into their motives, aims, sense of achievement, or unrealised ambition. The interviews published here for the first time took place between 1965–1980 when most of the authors were in their early or mid-career; their views and their convictions seen from a longer perspective of time remain critically valuable.

Print suffers from a defect compared with oral testimony: the reader cannot hear the tone, pitch, timbre, emphasis, the pauses which the tape recording (the basis of these conversations) reveals. On the other hand print ensures preservation and access to a wider audience, and allows the reader to consider and digest at leisure what passes by all too rapidly in sound. Here we can read within a broader context the writers' comments on their work, their careers where pursued outside the writing life, their attitudes to literature, to other writers, or simply to the transient experience of life itself.

All the texts are transcripts from the tapes. In the case of Ionesco the original French version is included along with the English translation. To avoid continuous repetition of the interviewer's and speakers' names in the margin of text, the convention has been to print the questions in italic type, the responses in roman type. In two cases a second person was present, hence the names are indicated. Thanks are due to the authors for permissions. Specific thanks are due to Alan Sillitoe and Virgin Publishing for permission to include his poem, 'Strategy and Statement,' and the opening page of *Saturday Night And Sunday Morning,* and to Carcanet Press for permission to include Hugh Macdiarmid's poems, 'The Watergow,' 'Crowdieknow' and 'Island Funeral.'

The date of each recording is given at the head of each interview.

The Writers

Stan Barstow (1966)

I'm sitting with Stan Barstow in Ossett, near Wakefield, which makes him one of the Northern group of writers because in Wakefield David Storey was brought up, and John Braine lives at Bingley, not very far away. Stan Barstow began his literary career with a novel, A Kind Of Loving, an instant success and filmed in 1960, since when he has written four books. Can we get the Northernness over with first? If I ask what does it mean to you to feel 'Northern' – is it a peculiar attitude you are conscious of or is it submerged in the literary creation?

I think this Northern thing is something we were all conscious of and can't be ignored, dating from the early days when we started to write; I say 'we' for a reason I'll come back to in a moment. It's true that *A Kind Of Loving* is the book that made the breakthrough for me, the first substantial piece of work of mine to be published, but I was writing for about eight or nine years before that with little success apart from one or two short stories being broadcast by the BBC. I was trying to write about the kind of life I knew, always a good thing for a writer to do, feeling isolated not knowing any other writers at all until about 1957 when *Room At The Top* was published and Keith Waterhouse's *There Is A Happy Land,* and only in 1960 did I learn of the existence of David Storey when his *This Sporting Life* came out just before *A Kind Of Loving.* The writers I've mentioned are sometimes spoken of as a group but the fact is that we didn't know each other and we were as surprised as anybody when we found we were quite so thick on the ground.

It is a phenomenon we would need to research deeply to find an answer to it: why did this happen just when it did? If you take the North as a whole then it would include Alan Sillitoe, Sid Chaplin, Stanley Middleton, Philip Callow, to mention just some who have started to make a mark in the past six or seven years. If you narrow it to the West Riding then that would mean John Braine, Storey, myself, and several writers just coming along now but who have yet to get established and have talent. If you narrow this even further and take just a little area as the back streets of Hunslet in Leeds, a real working class area of grim terraced houses, relics of the Industrial Revolution, and take just a few square yards of that district, out of that area in one generation came Richard Hoggart, Peter O'Toole, Keith Waterhouse and Willis Hall, and of those only Keith and Willis knew each other. It is a phenomenon that can't be ignored, that breakthrough of Northern writers, actors and so on. I think that illustrates just how many there are and how little involved with each other.

As far as my own writing is concerned I felt there was a great resistance against me in writing about what I knew from local experience, as if in some strange way my material was against me, resistance to the way in which I wanted to express what I felt because I was using material that people, readers, publishers were not particularly interested in: what was happening in the North. Now because of the big impact made by the work of all those writers, this has changed; films and novels have caused a swing back to the provinces, *but* since then, more recently there has been a reaction against the regions which were so popular, and in a sense we're now having the same questions put to us that were put to us before, with the implication that if you move to London and write about London then you will by some curious process produce more significant work. I haven't noticed this, and I don't like playing the North and South game except as a defence because I find I'm sometimes forced into playing it. I chose to stay here because the only other place I could go would be London, and I don't want to find myself in a close circle of writers and intellectuals. I like to keep my feet on the ground. I can find company of that kind around here when I want it and take it in the quantities I need while at the same time keep my feet on the ground among people who don't care about writing. It seems to me to be a better way to get to any material that is significant.

What I strongly resent is the implication that by writing about life in the West Riding I may somehow have robbed my work of any Universal Significance that it might find if I wrote about somebody else elsewhere. It seems to me that the only thing that will rob my work of significance is a failure on my part to make it significant enough or see it clearly enough. I prefer to plough a narrow furrow in depth than go out and mug up something I don't know. One point I always make to myself, a credo, is that you only get to the universal by a close examination of the particular. There are examples in front of us all the time now of international films which have no sense of place or character or real people but are a mish-mash of cultures, attitudes put out purely as entertainment, and I think there is a danger in trying to be too international and setting out deliberately to do this by broadening the scope of what one does in the wrong kind of way. So at least for the time being it's up to me to write as well as I can, to look as carefully as I can, to find the material and write about it in such a way that it will have relevance to people wherever they live.

2

In A Kind of Loving *you took the relationship between an immature young man and his fiancée and explored it thoroughly and candidly. Is this an accurate summary of that novel or were there other interests lying beneath the surface? I remember one critic saying, "if only Barstow had followed up the documentary aspects of the situation." I'm not quite sure what he meant, but I remember the comment and wondered if this was a reference to the environment?*

You would also find another critic – as a matter of fact I vaguely remember that comment and could probably find the review in my files – but there were many more critics, perhaps not about that book but certainly about the film and the general movement in the cinema at the time with films like *Room At The Top* and *Saturday Night And Sunday Morning* who saw both novels and films as documentary works, pieces of sociology. Now the furthest thing from my mind was to write a piece of sociology but what I like to do – and this must be pretty clear from what I've said – is to write about people, because it's the individuals I'm interested in and to see them in a definite environment, people who have been shaped by their environment, the places in which they live, by their "culture" in the broadest sense of the word. So I like to think that in everything I do there is a strong sense of place but I sincerely hope this would never overshadow the individuality of the people, and I think that the environment I know is more interesting for me than characters in the limbo of a London suburb. As a friend said to me recently "I'm sick of watching television plays about advertising men in London who are trying to find their souls". And that is what you are left with if you go to London and get into advertising. If you can't make a living by writing then that becomes the great subject and so becomes introspective, an incestuous way of writing – you are completely drawn in upon yourself. So I like to write about people with a strong sense of place who have been shaped by their environment and I wouldn't stress the documentary aspects of what I do. If I thought that was coming out strongly I would need to reassess what I was doing and find out why.

Motivation, behaviour and the deep springs of human action in human relations, these are what give you the stimulus to write?

Yes.

You have an extraordinary ear for dialogue and the nuances of expression used by local people. Is it a gift, the ability to do an exact mimicry but more than mimicry because there's spirit behind it?

It's strange to find myself saying this because I've read so many writers who have said it, namely that it is a clever imitation, but it's something that does come naturally, an ear for dialogue which you have or haven't . In the case of a section of life that I didn't know then I would have to develop it very consciously. If I were writing about an upper-class milieu I should have to listen first very attentively. As to the dialogue in my novels, I have been brought up amongst it and so instinctively I know it but the first thing to realise is that when it is written down it can't be put there as it rings inside one's head but has be put into readable form; if rendered phonetically besides being difficult reading it would make the characters sound much more ignorant than they actually are.

It was very well translated into screen terms, with Alan Bates and...

June Ritchie.

Both just right for the part. What is it like being involved in the filming of a novel?

Uncanny. Uncanny in the sense that for the first time you see your character clothed in flesh and they are not as you imagined them initially. It is different with a play because you realise that the characters are to be seen physically and there is always a dimension missing which the actors have to fill in. In the case of a novel which is a concrete thing in itself with its own life, as soon as the thing is cast then you become aware of approximations and compromises and you must rid your mind of everything but the requirements of the film and let it be the same object through a different medium. I can understand that some novelists can be very disturbed by the experience, but I found it exciting and I simply divorce the novel from the film; I look upon the film as a very good piece of work which doesn't overshadow the image of the novel in my own mind. The novel stays a novel.

As an author are you involved in the film? Do they consult you, or is it taken out of your hands in order to be re-created?

The main thing is that if you are asked to write the screenplay, as some of the writers we've mentioned – Sillitoe, Storey – have been, then obviously that means you are involved. I was invited to write the screenplay but for a number of reasons I said no, one of which was modesty since I thought it too difficult, though if the opportunity came again I don't think I would refuse, not because the screenplay was badly done but because I would have more confidence in my ability to do it. Once you say no, then strictly speaking you are written out of the contract; you take your money and that's it. After all, they can't have the novelist walking about on the set saying, "What's happened to Chapter Five?" A film is a film and the only criterion is that each should be good in its own way.

I found when I turned up on location on the few occasions when I did that they were nearly always discussing some point or other on which I could give an opinion and they would put their point of view and then do as they saw fit.

What about the writing life – you were for many years in an engineering firm? How does it compare with that life, which is presumably more routine and programmed? You are now comparatively a free spirit although clearly you must discipline yourself to the work. What kind of contrast have you found between the two different lives?

Firstly, you are on your own, and the essential thing to remember about writing is that although there can be a social life around you, and a working life if working in the theatre or television occasionally, it is all too easy to play at being a writer rather than doing the job itself. The essential thing to remember is that it does involve sitting on your own for long periods of time putting words on paper and there is no getting away from that simple isolation. This can be stimulating, frightening, depressing if the inspiration isn't coming. In my case what I do is on a long-term basis as opposed to a journalist, say, who writes his stories every day or each week. A novel may take me up to a year, then it will be another year before it is published and a further year before any real money comes in from it, but provided you are financially safe for a while it is all too easy to put off until tomorrow what you should be doing today. Thinking that today doesn't matter, and I'm often guilty of this. It would be easy to fall into a rut whereby you are not actually working, finding excuses for not working, so that it is essential to set up similar hours as those you spent when in a salaried post. When you work in an office what you do is to some extent dependent on others: somebody will pass you a piece of paper which needs action, or the telephone rings and you must respond, or someone will come to ask you about some piece of business and you have to do something about it. There is no such routine in writing; you sit down with a piece of paper in the typewriter or under your pen and if you do nothing about that, there – that's the end of it. And it's easy to continue week after week without doing anything about it. The point is that you have to be firm, and this brings us to the basic discipline of the job.

You have to discipline yourself when it doesn't come easy to make it come because although the thing called inspiration is quite a valid fact of life it doesn't come simply out of the blue but out of a climate of work, out of a morning when you didn't know how to get the first sentence down but you put something down, then another sentence, then a paragraph, and the paragraph led to a page, and one page to another, and out of this, people walking and talking and moving on paper, will come the spark that set it alight and makes it move along to some purpose, in the direction in which you hope it will move. But this is something a writer must work out for himself and it's easy to overlook such basics; I may say that I'm guilty of all the faults I've mentioned including another fault: wanting too much in my head. I'm not the kind of writer who can think out his story too far or too closely ahead – I have to make it work on paper and I am guilty of wanting too much to happen, so that I'll walk about the room, look out of the window, write a letter, poke my pipe out, clean the typewriter, anything rather than get that first vital sentence down on paper and then make that sentence become two.

Do you need to go out into the world to refresh your sources of inspiration and find the material or do you feel you have now sufficient to carry on?

I don't think it is ever as conscious as this! Living in an environment I've always known though not now directly in that environment since I've moved up in the social scale – I live in better conditions than those I've lived in as a boy but of course I am still in contact with the background I've always known. I'm fairly gregarious and like to go out, particularly after spending all day on my own; it's nice to go to the pub and talk to people or over to Leeds and talk to my friend in the BBC there. These are all ways in which while enjoying myself and refreshing myself I'm also living, and consciously absorbing other matters to be used. I never consciously look for copy, though I would check certain facts if they were necessary to the work in order to be realistic, authentic, but I would never go to a place in the hope that there would be a story there or seek out particular people. It's simply a matter of living and hoping that something will come out of it, some work will develop from it.

Do you see in the man/woman relationship a central situation which is worth analysis and treatment? Since Lawrence, this is very important isn't it?

Understanding the sexual relationship in the deepest possible way, an influence which has spread throughout fiction. Is this valid for you and will you make it the basis for exploration?

I think that's true. Somewhere in the middle of all I do there's a man/woman relationship. How can I put it? If I'm in a room full of people who are talking politics I'd be much more interested if I caught sight of a man looking at a woman across the room or a woman looking at a man and I could see a spark of something there. What they were thinking would be much more interesting to me than all the idle speculation about party politics, or general social issues. The sort of situation that is basic to life whatever we do with the world. Somewhere along the way there will be social comment, certain political or religious attitudes will break through because of course the action continues in a particular society, and what the man and woman say to each other is not in a vacuum. Can I put it this way: the man is what he is partly through personality and partly the result of a shaping environment. They may have problems in their relationship which are created by the environment which a similar couple in another context would not experience and it's that which fascinates me. Men and women will go on wrestling with problems which can be recognised and responded to by people in any situation. Personal relationships, or simply being human, is fascinating to me and although I won't come up with the answers I hope to set out the problems in an interesting and constructive way.

Two final questions: man is often described as an isolated creature nowadays. It is fashionable to think of him as an alien in an alien universe without his old beliefs and relationships and the destruction of the old ways of life. Do you agree with this?

I do in one sense: I do agree that man is lonely, that each person is a prisoner within his or her own skin, bounded by their own personality, and that people go to literature as a form of consolation, to be reassured that other people are like them, that they are valid human beings. I think that man may have rested too much on institutions in the past and used these as a substitute for real commitment and communication between himself and his fellows. Now the institutions are breaking down and we need to look to our fellow men more and more, since we are more dependent on each other and we must be more dependent on each other. I think it true to say that there is more moral concern today in the world than there ever has been despite the terrible atrocities that have happened. My hope is that this moral concern may assume a more valid form in person to person communication without sanctions or institutional beliefs, codes and rules imposed upon people.

And your own reading – what kind of influences, what kind of literary sources prompted you to write?

My reading was fairly haphazard and when I started to write I was looking round for some justification for writing and for the first few years H.E. Bates was the writer who showed me what a short story could be, and what a pure novelist was, and gave me a great deal of inspiration without knowing it by his professional example. I went on to others of course; no writer from my background can escape the influence of Lawrence, and there are writers of my own generation I find stimulating, but Bates was *the* writer and I read his stuff from the 1930s; he was the one who put me on the straight and narrow, and whenever I want to get my bearings I go back to the things that he has written. His biography of Edward Garnett* is very good with a number of pertinent things to say, and so has his *Modern Short Story*, about what writing ought to be; many of his comments I don't agree with but in almost everything he says there is a kernel of truth which I can get hold of and so continue to keep my feet on the ground.

———————— ◆•◆ ————————

*Edward Garnett (1950)

8

Edmund Blunden and Vernon Scannell

(1966)

Edmund Blunden and Vernon Scannell are two English poets who belong to the generation of the First World War and immediately after in the case of Edmund Blunden, and Vernon Scannell to the post-Second World War. Edmund Blunden has recently been made Professor of Poetry at Oxford, which Chair he will hold for five years from 1965. When did you first publish?

Blunden   In 1914, just after the outbreak of war, at least that was the first little book I published.[1]

And you then wrote Undertones Of War *which, like Robert Graves'* Goodbye To All That, *became a classic of the First World War?*

Blunden   That came out a little later, after the war, I think in 1928. There had been a number of war books, like R.H. Mottram's[2], and then Graves' about the same time as mine. I think most of them appeared about ten years after, though A.P. Herbert's *The Secret Battle* was already out, in 1919.

Do you consider yourself a traditionalist, whatever that means?

Blunden   I haven't thought much about that, though I think I could hardly be otherwise, since I have a strong sense against new ideas creeping into one's head and of new forms taking too much hold, but I don't think of myself as necessarily writing in any tradition unless it be a general tradition experimenting as one goes.

Would you say, for example, that after the First World War, when you came back, you felt excited by what T.S. Eliot was doing, or did you find that what you had been doing beforehand conditioned you and carried you on as an individual?

Blunden   I was always struck by *Prufrock*, though *The Waste Land* didn't work on me for quite some time, but that was because there were all sorts of ways of looking at life. I forget when I began to

[1]*Poems* (1914)

[2]*A Personal Record* (1929)

9

know that poem as well as one should know it but it didn't at the time move me as much as other writers. It was some time before my sort of experience faded away behind his which was so well done in the poem

Vernon Scannell, if I can turn to you now. Edmund Blunden is alleged to have said when he took over the Chair of Poetry late in 1965, "If I can make a few people less hostile to poetry after my five years in the Chair I will be happy." What kind of success do you think any poet can have in that sort of ambition nowadays? Convincing people poetry has something for them.

Scannell   I'm not very optimistic. It is a form of literature which makes greater demands than any other; therefore, fewer people are willing to face those demands, and all the easy undemanding means of communication, like television, are naturally to be set against poetry.

What about your own experience as a poet, which came out of the Second World War? Did it seem to you the only possible kind of life – was there anything evangelical about it? Were you part of a movement?

Scannell   No, I've never been part of a movement and certainly not of The Movement which emerged in the 1950s. In fact there was a little anthology called *Maverick* which as the title suggests were poets one could call outsiders. Even so, I don't think there was a Movement, but just a journalistic stunt, and I think we are all simply poets trying to find a way of expressing things in the best possible way.

To say things 'in the best possible way' should mean that you ought to be able to reach a wider audience the more sophisticated people become. Have you both found this as you have travelled around the country giving recitals? Is this happening or does the minority interest in poetry not seem to grow any greater? How do you feel, Edmund Blunden?

Blunden   I'm impressed by the numbers of people present in audiences, and the attention given, and the questions have been strong and deep. How far this is a novelty, I don't know, but the type of audience we're getting now is better than the ones I can recall when I was first trying to read and lecture on poetry – or rather, talk on the subject – after World War One. I think there is improvement in the regard paid to poetry and the hope is that readings will be useful to the general reader. We've had mixed audiences but when there are a hundred present then ninety-nine are actually writers – I'm not sure about the percentage!

Is this the sense you got from your audiences – that they consisted of people who wrote or were anxious to be writers?

Blunden   It might well be so, but we haven't tested it.

Were they young?

Blunden   The last two were young, certainly.

Scannell   But mixed – there were middle aged of both sexes, some elderly, some very young. In Alfreton here the other day there were schoolchildren and it was from them that the best questions came.

I wonder if that means that poetry is becoming more a part of the experience of the child today, in school? Is that likely?

Blunden   We always had to memorise poems in my own schooldays, and be acquainted with the names of our poets, though not so much contemporary writers. That is the difference between those days and the situation today.

Scannell   Yes, that is where the progress is so marked. There are a number of anthologies of purely contemporary poets' work used in secondary modern schools, some of excellent quality, one called *Here Today* issued with a long-playing record of the poets reading their poems in the anthology. One hopes that might help a little, but in Manchester, for instance, we performed in a room which was full but the room was a little room, and if you consider the population of Manchester, that is not many. One in five thousand would be a pretty good figure!

11

Can you discern what is happening to poetry today? You mentioned The Movement, Vernon Scannell, which was poetry fairly lucid, of straightforward statement, Philip Larkin-type poetry, and that seemed to make an impact. Larkin himself occupies quite a niche, and seems welcomed by a large readership but so many poets in the past few years are highly introspective, highly wrought, with sophisticated minds – Jon Silkin, for instance, or John Holloway. Is this significant, or is it just something that happens?

Scannell   I suppose that's true, it's got to happen, but I myself do not like abstraction in literature. I like a poem to have a core, a centre of recognisable experience, in the broader sense a narrative centre, though the narrative core may be submerged; it needn't be a narrative poem.

Is this what you try to do in your own work?

Scannell   Yes, it is.

Who is your own favourite among existing poets – is it possible to say? Or influence?

Scannell   I don't think any direct influence, though Auden is the biggest general influence on all poets of my generation, a considerable poet with a wide-ranging mind.

How do you feel, Edmund Blunden, about meeting audiences?

Blunden   A novelty for me since I've usually been a lecturer on a platform, but this is a pleasant way in which two reading lives are questioned as well as the readers, and it is a more active way of coming to the art of poetry myself than if I simply stand there and give a formal talk. Perhaps the views are the same but they have to be expressed in relation to someone else's feelings – Vernon Scannell's – with which I didn't take the bearings until we met on this occasion; there was no time to compare notes, and that was good for both of us and for the hearers. I don't think I can do without publishing something, now and again, in the void.

Scannell   Yes, I think that's important. To me the poem is the words on the page. One likes to see people going round to poetry recitals, and when I was in Edinburgh last August people like Betjeman and Auden, big public figures were reading and people were being turned away. I felt then that it was a personality cult among the audience, and another point about public readings: one tends, and I find other poets agree, to read less characteristic poems, less good poems because they make greater impact.

Is the work on the radio effective? I think you have been involved with the Third Programme? Do you get any comeback from that? Letters, comments from listeners? Does there seem to be a listening audience?

Scannell   Oh yes, there is, and I think in terms of mass communications it is a small one but a discerning one, and the letters, apart from the fringe ones which do come, are very interesting. In fact I'd say it is one of the rewards of writing that one receives letters out of the blue, rather like sending messages out to sea in a bottle and hoping they'll be washed up on some friendly shore.

Malcolm Bradbury *(1980)*

So far Malcolm Bradbury has written three novels: Eating People Is Wrong, *Stepping Westward and* The History Man *in addition to a considerable body of criticism and humorous collections. To a living professor of English (and of American) Literature who writes fiction the first question has to be: how far does your creative work conflict with your critical work? I'm thinking of Leavis's comment about queering one discipline with the habits of another. Can you keep them apart?*

It's a difficult relationship. Part of the task is to learn to make the break between being a critic into being a writer. I ritualise this break by being part of my life in a university and part outside it. I now teach part-time at the university of East Anglia, so that for six months of the year I am a teacher and critic and for the other six months I am a novelist and reviewer, and that specific dramatisation of the separation is important to me, but as far as I'm concerned I would not like to live solely by writing. I don't know if there is a full answer to this but I certainly do get a lot from criticism and teaching, for my novels. The kind of novels I have started to write over recent years have been shaped by critical theory and I think that is true of fiction in general – there is a move towards a more speculative and experimental fiction in most countries including Britain and mine have tended in that direction, shaped by recent criticism.

Criticism is not a fixed thing, of course. You mentioned Leavis, and we are conducting this interview in Downing College, Cambridge, Leavis's college where his shadow lies heavily, but Leavis was a critic of a particular generation and particular flavour, a critic whose work no doubt did influence my first two novels which are written in the tradition of moral realism and that moral realism is precisely what one had to look for in fiction. More recently criticism has gone much further into the study of language, semiotics – sign systems – and more concerned with the writer as the producer of a text and literature as a written thing engaging with the reader in a peculiarly uncertain way fugitive way.

Is that called Structuralism?

Structuralism is part of that; more latterly it has been called Post-Structuralism, Deconstruction. Those things do affect me. The question in the end is *how?* The last thing I would do is to sit down to write a

Leavisian novel or a Post-Structuralist novel, nonetheless my sense of what it is to be a writer is shaped by those ideas. The curious thing is that one is conscious, and one imbibes, what is debated in classroom discussions and this remanifests itself when next one is doing creative writing; at the same time no good writer would write according to a theory.

Another important factor in your work is that you are a comic novelist, a rare species, one who sees the world in mock heroic or humorous terms. Would that be fair?

Yes, I am certainly a comic novelist, and just as in the nearly thirty years since I began writing, critical views have changed, so the kind of comedy has changed as well. My first two novels were in the tradition of comedy that is very English, indeed the English novel started as comedy in the works of my two heroes: Henry Fielding, author of *Tom Jones*, and Laurence Sterne, author of *Tristram Shandy*; I do see a strong tradition of comedy. But in my first two novels the comedy was more like Fielding's, social and moral, concerned with a purgation of hypocrisy and with examination of the absurdities of the moral life. My more recent writing, *The History Man*, and the novel I'm writing now called *Rates Of Exchange* is more influenced by Sterne's view of life, comedy put to a different purpose, much more concerned with absurdity, that social life does not give us a safe and subjective basis for a moral life; in some fashion my comedy has become less moral because I'm less sure about my moral position.

Your anti-hero Louis Bates in Eating People Is Wrong *is a very different creature from Howard Kirk in* The History Man.

Indeed: there are two central figures in *Eating People Is Wrong*, Louis Bates, a mature but youngish student who comes to a provincial university and embarrasses the faculty there, and the professor, Professor Treece, a liberal figure left over from the 1930s, himself embarrassed by being in the 1950s and in the provinces – almost one and the same thing, a man caught between two contradictions, a Thirties political attitude and a Fifties moral attitude, and is extremely anxious about his liberalism. What I was trying to set out in that book was the morality of liberalism, its absurdities and also its strengths; I do think him absurd but not necessarily foolish. Howard Kirk in *The History Man* is an adversary figure from right the other end of the spectrum, a radical sociologist opposed to the liberalism and humanism you might associate with my earlier characters, for me a new kind of hero requiring a new kind of writing to deal with 'him. The point there is that the liberal character has been displaced to the fringes while this powerful new type is at the centre of the action, both historically assertive and in some ways also corrupt, so my comedy is less warm, engulfing comedy surrounding these characters.

You have written extensively for television: Love On A Gunboat *and* The After-Dinner Game, *again much of it placed within an academic milieu. Does this mean you can test the world outside and plumb its absurdities and hypocrisies by using the academic scene? Is it just as valid as, say, the business world or the buccaneers in politics?*

I think it is. I know there are many who think it separate from everyday life, self-enclosed, which is quite untrue because while it shares the facts of everyday life it is also an analytical environment, and I suppose I like writing about intelligent, doubtful people who are concerned with what I consider are very contemporary issues. Because these people are in a university they confront those issues in a certain typical way, with ideas, articulating what they think in a way that people in the hard economic world outside would not do.

As you continue in university teaching has your sense of helplessness in the face of what is happening malevolently in the world grown? You spoke about the change of ethos in your comedy – does this mean it is growing more melancholy, less robust?

I think it does mean it is growing more melancholy. All my work is pessimistic but one can be pessimistic about many different issues, and in the earlier books there is a good bit about the incapacity of people in Britain in the 1950s to free themselves from a rather confining world-view; Britain in that era was a narrow, self-satisfied, little-English kind of country, so that there the drive is towards a hope of greater openness, freedom. By the end of the Sixties when I started writing *The History Man* my pessimism was quite different as the liberalism which I had always valued and satirised was disappearing under the onslaught of an anti-humanist world-view, which is not just that of the extreme Left but is also under the pressure of a new image which has come to possess us of man as an infinitely exposed creature. Our psychological life is explicable out of Freud, our political life out of Marx, our life at any level is open to deterministic interpretations, and at the same time we have become increasingly conscious of ourselves as victims of history which is to say that whenever we perform as human beings we are conscious all the time of living now, that people living now act in a certain way, can buy a style of life, and nothing seems to suggest that there is a separate, autonomous person, a moral decider, within the human being, which is transcendent, stands outside and somehow judges all this. Thus it means that if you are eighteen you have to decide whether you are a skinhead or a mod, if you're middle aged you have to choose between the male or female menopause, and all these things appear to be structured as a cultural proposition, and we define our lives by this kind of fashionable history. This is a very important theme in *The History Man* for me. In that sense it is the disappearance of the subject, of the autonomous self, that is the object of pessimism, and is the theme of the book I am writing now.

I mentioned your work on television, and your most popular novel, The History Man *was successfully televised. Do you feel comfortable in this medium both as a writer for television and as a writer who has been adapted for the screen?*

I certainly enjoy writing plays for television…

Do they take very long to write?

Far less long than a novel, but then a novel takes me about ten years! So they seem much shorter to do, mainly because they are commissioned and are due by a certain date. They require a lot of hard work over a specified period, about three months or so, and then more hard work when they start to get made, when in rehearsal it becomes clear that some scenes don't actually work. I think television fascinates me because it is very much *not* like writing fiction – it is a large collaborative enterprise, and that is an experience that has to be learned carefully. Learning collaboration means learning all over again, learning what instruments are available for use; as a novelist I feel pretty professional and understand the manipular elements of a novel, point of view or tense, or length; there are certain classic laws or standards which you can acquire and improve by making yourself more expert in these. In television you must start all over again, thinking about giving actors performances and certain kinds of performances suited to a small screen, remembering where the camera is because the camera is a point of vision (as Henry James would say) of a very complex kind, not the same kind as the angle of vision in fiction.

So all the various elements in television must be in mind: the set, the actors, the director and kind of direction likely, the camera angles, the use of visual image – the main use of TV is not with words. Slowly and the hard way all these factors have to be learned , and I think my television plays are becoming more professional and getting better. *The History Man* was not adapted by myself but by Christopher Hampton, and I thought very well done. The effect of an intervening writer and the presence of an interesting director whom I know and who has directed plays I have written – given this degree of intervention the object is quite different. The novel is a long way from a television series and I am not unhappy about that condition because I've been pleased with my work as seen on television. It is simply the transmission of one thing neatly into other terms.

Have you found a reciprocity between writer, director, actors? Actors strike me nowadays as more intelligent than they used to be.

Oh that's certainly true! One of the virtues of being a writer in Britain is the ready access for a writer who takes himself seriously, as I'm afraid I do, to a medium which is used in quite different ways; in other words a serious play can actually work on television in Britain whereas in other countries it couldn't, America for instance, where writing for television is genre writing and done to a formula. Of course serious writing can be to a formula but in Britain such a writer can use television in a way which is creative acting, indeed acting now is adapted to the actuality of the text, not tied into a bland nothingness. The way television drama is made ensures that every play in a good series like *Play For Today* has its own laws, its own writer and has to do many different things.

Turning to English studies and criticism now, though I know your primary interest is now in American literature, the seriousness you referred to was true of the 1950s under the influence of Leavis, the strenuous claims he made on behalf of literary study as a great moral experience. There seems to be a reaction against this, that English is not necessarily the centrality that Leavis insisted it was, that there are many routes to the truth, and that English may even be displaced. Do you have the feeling that it is not dethroned, but in danger of something like that?

That danger has been around for a long time. As Leavis dominated the Fifties so a variety of new versions of English studies came through in the Sixties, and there was an overthrowing of many of the attitudes we call the

New Criticism; the subject did start to remake itself in the 1960s and 1970s. The change came from several directions, one from an increase in professionalisation. Leavis seems to me to dramatise the sensitive but nonetheless realistic reader who is responding to a text by trying to draw values out of it, and of course at the other end of that exchange must be a writer who invests values in the text, who somehow celebrates valuable and worthwhile things which humanistically make life important. In the 1960s there was a tendency to de-moralise texts, to take away that moral exchange, and this form of de-moralisation is like all such de-moralisation, demoralising! It has been obvious that it produces disappointment in students, and in that sense it made me anxious.

To make this a little clearer: the great switch in the Sixties was towards criticism which was more linguistically based, the study of a literary text as a linguistic performance, a language *act*. In this sense there is little material difference in taking a Tolstoy novel or a Barbara Cartland novel or a piece of newspaper prose for study: it is the presence of writing that is significant, not the writer or reader. English has been caught up in that problem ever since the Sixties, and because of it the study of English literature has taken on ideas from subjects which help one to think about those ideas – linguistics, anthropology, to some extent some of the sciences, psychology, so that during the Seventies a much more professionalised subject has developed, much more theoretical, with a sense of ambiguity about literature: we don't know what the canon is, which are the best books to study, we have no way of making up that canon. We don't know either what constitutes the safe terms of the classic description of, say, the novel. The writer becomes an ambiguous figure, the text becomes an ambiguous object, the reader becomes a mystery, so that about all the elements of the exchange between the writer and reader questions are asked and many of these have done much to reshape writing. And this takes us back to the first question you asked about the relationship between the writer and the critic; there is no doubt that many of these ideas produce a new climate which anyone seriously interested in writing cannot avoid because this language-act has been rescored in some real fashion.

All this is important but the difficulty is in the loss of that classic attachment which has existed since antiquity between an engaged writer and an engaged reader, that classic transcendental sympathy between an author and reader, that is, an engaged writer and an engaged reader where the book is being used as readers wished it to be used in a moralistic way to help people know more about life and to understand what it is that the writer has to offer, as a power, a force, an alternative, in a culture which to many of us is becoming increasingly depressing. Culture over the past thirty years has grown more materialistic, more vulgar, adrift within itself, unsure of its intentions, more divided, more stagnant, recessive, defeated, tired.

Given the ideas you have mentioned, the new approaches since the Sixties, is it possible to be as collaborative in class as Leavis always insisted one should be? That the study of texts was a process of collaboration – "This is so, isn't it?" – is that possible within the new constraints? Or is it more likely in the new analytical climate?

At one end there is an intensification of textual study, which Leavis was much concerned with, so it is possible to elicit more from a text than Leavis ever did, precisely because there are more resources open to us from semiotics or linguistic theory which enable us to talk more exactly and fully about the constitution of a story – we can see more clearly what went into its making and the way in which it relates to other texts as well; there is in the end a peculiar sameness about stories, in other words a narrative grammar. At the other end there is a temptation to dispense with the literary text altogether, that is, the kind of criticism which takes the text as a pretext for its own activities, and in a curious way the creative work becomes a secondary object, and the activity of criticism becomes the primary object, a kind of philosophical discourse conducted in class when you leave behind the particular literary text that began the occasion because what you are really doing is engaging in complex premises about the nature of language, and the disappearance of the text is part of that general disappearance of the subject. As a writer I see that as a threat. As a teacher, too, I see it is threatening to a degree because in the end I see the study of literature as the study of very good books and the pursuit of the moral, creative reasons which make one say they are very good books.

Will fiction bend or buckle under this sort of approach? Is it going to turn into something else? Documentary? Norman Mailer's books are somewhere between fiction and factual journalism. Does this matter?

I think the real change is a change in realism, that is to say in the years after the war it seemed as if realism was coming back. Realism I think of as a creative compact, a writer assuming he can appeal to readers in an act of recognition; that a reader will recognise that what the author says is real is so, that it is like the world the reader experiences. Now there seems to be a vacating of many of the assumptions of realism, and that vacating leads in different directions: it might lead to intensification of documentary writing, greater naturalism, but often this documentary is extremely conscious of its fictional character. Mailer is an interesting example: his book *Armies of the Night*, with its double subtitle "Fiction As History" and "History As Fiction," is determined to show rightly that all accounts of a so-called "true" experience are fictional. His is consciously fictional because he is a novelist, but the press's accounts are unconsciously fictional, and Mailer, like many people also who work in television, knows that the so-called "realities" that they transmit are the result of chance shots or are selected from the chaos and contingency of a larger experience. Or is actually affected by the camera being there in the first place, so that fictionality is occurring by the intrusion of the artist or the camera or the documenter into a given situation.

So, unitive innocence doesn't seem to be available as it once was, and I think this has become a commonplace of most writing, in fiction, in the theatre, and it always was a commonplace in poetry. What we have moved away from is that realistic illusion of the 1950s, which is a striking change, not a change which need worry us in itself because it is a change which has happened many times before – literature has visited and then left realism – realism is an episode rather than the nature of literature. There have been many "realisms"; most movements, some ostensibly unrealistic, in the end think they are dealing with Reality, but Reality and realism are not the same thing.

Perhaps we can close by talking about your own working methods. You mentioned that it does take you along time to write a novel, but you are a busy Head of Department which must shut out any possibility of concentration during term time. Does this mean you work in vacations or on sabbaticals, or can you go home at the weekend and say, "Right, four hours today, Saturday and Sunday."?

No. I separate out my writing activities from my teaching and critical activities, and in fact I'm not a Head of Department (for which I'm thankful) but I am a professor and teach two-thirds of the year. I don't administer, and so during that period I mix teaching and criticism. When I go home at the weekend that enables me to write criticism, for example most recently a book on modern American fiction*, but as far as the novel

The Modern American Novel (1983)

is concerned that does have to be isolated because it's almost a psychic change in my temperament, and I can only manage to live with a novel if I live with it continuously, without interruption or without serious interruption, something pressing hard on me, as teaching must do. So for that part of the year when I'm a writer, about six months of the year now, I concentrate purely on fiction and I work by sitting down at a typewriter beginning on what is left over from the previous day, continuing to write until about six in the evening. Much of that is rewriting since I'm an obsessive rewriter, and having started a chapter, well before I've finished it I feel the need to go over it time and time again...

Before advancing further?

Sometimes I will advance further, but more commonly not. The first revision is stylistic – I'm trying to refine the sentences – and I do believe that writing a novel is not unlike writing a poem in the sense that I'm concerned to invigilate every word that I use, as a poet does, and must do. There's enormous concern that what I have to say is expressed properly, and at the same time it's more than stylistic because it's a process of going back into the words and to reimagine them and reimagining why they were there in the first place. The more I go back the more the book changes, so that you become aware that you are not writing the book you thought you were in the first place; it is a different book, and as that understanding comes it changes everything in the whole novel.

A specific of the example of that is *The History Man*. There were various reasons why I thought it best to tell the story in the present sense but I didn't realise that until I had been working on it for quite a long time and so had to throw away a lot of material that wasn't written in the present tense. Once the present tense is decided on, it isn't simply a matter of changing all the verbs in the past tense because the two tenses don't function in the same way – the field of the tense is quite different, so I was dismissing a large amount of work already done and beginning again. Many of the events I had written in the past tense, indeed every one of them, had to be refigured. So a novel for me is a very slow process, one of writing and rewriting and of intensive composition which goes on over a long period of time and because it goes on over so long a period it tends to digest the time itself – that is to say part of what it's about is taking a long time to write it – if that makes sense.

The History Man was a book I started in the late Sixties and I set it in the year in which it was written but with each new year I kept changing the year, and if that changes then everything changes. Only by driving it forward in that way and trying to digest a whole period of recent social time was I able to a understand what the book was really about. It was about the deep-seated social change, something which has since changed again. It came out in 1975 and is very much a dated book from my point of view except that it has its own interest from the fact of its being dated. I hope it's also dateless or timeless. The same is true of the book I'm writing now which is set in 1977, but 1977 has to ingest as it were 1978, 1979, 1980 and the other years in which I've been writing.

Do you use notebooks?

Yes, but not in the sense that I bring them with me to parties and sit in the lavatories jotting notes down on things seen and heard. I used to do that – I did it during the first two novels. Now the notebooks are used when I'm sitting on trains, working out ideas or rephrasing sentences already written. I sit there staring out at cows, rethinking them.

Is there any likelihood that your teaching and critical work will impinge too much on your creative work or will you continue to continue to compartmentalise them because of nearly thirty years of experience behind you?

I'd like to continue in the same schizophrenic way, but one wonders what will become of universities after the recent educational cuts announced by the present Conservative government, which seem to me to be tragic and ill considered and which will do considerable intellectual damage to the university and the community. The future of universities in the Eighties is going to be far more depressing and unnerving than that in the Sixties or Seventies, and it may be that the university is no place to be. What I fear most is a disastrous provincialism. Having mildly castigated the Conservative government I would go on to mention the folly of coming out of the Common Market for exactly the same reason, in other words there seems to be a drive towards provincialism, protective provincialism, in English culture which is taking us back to some of the views of the 1950s when provincialism was in sway, something which is not good for any culture at all.

John Braine (1966)

On a gusty Yorkshire day I'm in Bingley in the West Riding, almost the home town of John Braine, a territory new to me, but having seen the banks and braes around here I can see the force of the title of his first novel, Room At The Top: *there is a hill which looks very like " 't Top" looming above this road. It's now nine years since that novel was published, an overnight success which became a byword. Looking back on it now after nine years as a novelist, what are your feelings about it?*

I should say unmixed gratitude, although having lived with it for all those years it's difficult to escape from *Room At The Top*. It often happens with authors: writing a book which is enormously popular – it may not be the first one – and for ever afterwards you are known as the author of that one book, which is at times hard to bear and makes you feel like screaming out loud. I have written three other books since, two of which were very different. Still, if that's a complaint then, as they say in America, "I should have your complaint!"

The theme of Room At The Top *was, I suppose, the traditional Rags To Riches theme, but in a keenly contemporary atmosphere in which Joe Lampton's fight took place. Was this something you had picked up from the Yorkshire environment or was it a subject which interested you from your own reading which you wanted to rework and redevelop?*

It's a very common theme and occurs again and again, not really a present day theme at all but a fairy story, the tale of the swineherd and the princess. The curious thing is that some critics refer to me as a regional novelist when the point is that a novel has to be set somewhere – London is just as much a region as the West Riding, and it would be as parochial to write exclusively about London as about the West Riding. But that novel has appealed to readers all over the world, in countries wildly different from England, so I conclude that it must be universal in its appeal. In Russia *Room At The Top* has been hugely popular because in Russia there are Joe Lamptons and Papa Browns, rich father in-laws; I've visited Russia twice and there the class differences are sharper than they are here. In Russia income tax is 15% of income, so there is a curious situation that it's at the same level, there is also an absolutely Victorian atmosphere there, a Victorian moral code, so that for the writer, Russia would be a better place to live in than this country which has too much of this damned equality. Russia would be a far better place from the point of view of the novelist if only – and this is important – the novelist were free to write exactly as he pleases. But I'm not going into political questions – I'm not interested in politics at this stage.

Since Room At The Top *you have written* The Vodi, Life At The Top *and* The Jealous God. Life At The Top *was roughly handled by the critics – was this because they thought you were flogging a dead horse? Milking the applause? Doing too much with the same theme? How did you feel about that?*

As for the critics – that was to be expected. *Life At The Top* is a very different novel from *Room At The Top;* different in atmosphere, and it tries to do something which most English novels never begin to attempt, whether or not it succeeded. I wanted to portray properly the relationship between parent and child, particularly *father* and child, and I wanted to be realistic about the whole business of money and "success." I didn't want to give the impression that Joe was discontented with his success; he was discontented because he wasn't as successful as he thought he would be, a quite different issue. Critics, most of them, are predictable. I'm reading a book by an American psychiatrist, Dr Bergler[1], which was attacked by reviewers but which when I read it I was astonished to find made telling points, a good book, and without going into the details of Bergler's thesis one of the points he makes is this: that the majority of reviewers are failed authors, and that is so true – they are failed authors, and their instinct is, conscious as they are of their failure, to be more vicious with creative authors, the better the author the more vicious they are, the more they want to pull him down. When they praise they prefer to praise a mediocrity because as Bergler says, they have no reason to be jealous of a mediocrity. One of the things which gives me great pleasure is the fact that so many reviewers have written novels which have been flops – I think of Kenneth Allsop who is not as bad as the rest, a man of reasonable intelligence, not as vicious as the others because he has achieved success on television, an ephemeral medium, and is fairly well off. Allsop has written a few novels himself, all of which have been flops or which at best might just have cleared their advance. Then I think of John Coleman – if I mention his name now this will be the only publicity it will ever get – who

[1]*The Writer And Psychoanalysis* (1951)

is regularly bitter about me and drags in snide references to me even when not reviewing my books. I seem to be on his mind more than somewhat, and it's on my mind too that back in 1959 it was announced that Mr John Coleman was writing a novel; the curious thing is that one hasn't heard of this novel being published, and I'm in the presence of a librarian who would be aware of such a novel appearing, and I myself always know about all fiction that is published, it always sticks in my mind, so one concludes from this that he hasn't finished the novel or he has finished it and it has been turned down. You even come across this in reasonably successful writers like Penelope Mortimer when recently in the *New Statesman* in the course of praising a novel which one may be sure was mediocre chose to praise it in terms of dispraise of me. I thought this rather gratuitous but then I reflected that I must be in Miss Mortimer's mind far more often than she is in mine.

That sort of thing is a little hard to bear. I wouldn't say it hurts me, and it doesn't stop one from writing what one wants to write, nor do I think it makes any difference at all to my standing with the public, but it's like someone spitting in your face. It doesn't hurt but it makes you feel dirty. So, one did expect this kind of thing with *Life At The Top,* and it's one of the things one has to endure, something every major writer of my generation has had to put up with.

To dispense with the question of criticism and your novels, let's take the last one, The Jealous God, *which was on the whole received favourably, with the suggestion that John Braine has found himself, that this was more like it. Would this affect you at all? When they applaud you, or were you surprised at this kind of reaction?*

It would be futile to deny that it didn't please one to be praised, but you know the odd thing about being a writer is that even when you are generally praised there are some idiots who didn't praise you, which takes the gilt off the gingerbread. You tend to think they didn't praise you enough or that they praised the wrong things, so I suppose the moral is as Hemingway put it, that the great danger for any writer is to believe the critics when the say you're good or when they say you're bad. Two dangers to avoid. What you have to try to do is school yourself to be indifferent to the critics, except to be guided by the feelings of the few people whose opinions you value, and there will never be many of those. And always their opinions will coincide with your own, so that even their opinions are superfluous.

What about your working methods? You were writing for some time before that first success, and you had given up your job as a librarian in order to write.

I quit work as a librarian in 1951 but had to return to it in 1954, and left it again in 1957 when *Room At The Top* came out. I wouldn't recommend any would-be writer to do that; I could only do it myself because I wasn't then married. It would be insane for any married man to attempt to do it, and indeed as things are at present I think it ridiculous for anyone to try to earn a living as a full-time writer; I can think of nothing more stupid. It isn't possible to exist as a writer unless you are extremely successful because unless you are a hack – nothing wrong with being a hack, useful and necessary – then financial insecurity would destroy you as a writer. You cannot be a good writer unless you have a skin too few, and if you grow an extra skin, harden yourself, you will stop yourself from being a true writer. But yes, I do have professional ways of working. I work in this flat which is near my home from nine to five each day, a place where I can work in peace and quiet. I couldn't possibly work at home because I now have three children, two of them very small, each under two years old. Without having a huge house in which you could seal yourself off it's impossible to work at home, and even then it isn't a good idea.

Do any particular subjects claim your attention? Before you embark on a novel do you do a lot of reading either desultorily or purposively, then get the typewriter out, put in the paper and get going, or does your mind roam on current problems like the struggle towards success or as in the last novel, Jealous God, *problems of faith and morals? You are a Roman Catholic: does this present you with ready-made topics or do you not see yourself as a member of any particular sect but as a person open and receptive to possible subjects?*

As a writer I think of myself as like the ideal librarian: no religion, no politics, no morals. I see things not in terms of abstract ideas but simply in terms of people and dramatic situations. As for research, I do try to get the facts right, and do a certain amount of research before I begin a novel but after that my point of view is that I must get on with the story and if some facts need checking, do it afterwards. I'm not the Emile Zola kind of novelist, filling up whole notebooks with details. I haven't the idea of presenting a huge, composite picture of contemporary life: I think it would come out dead. On the other hand I like to get the facts right, and as to the question of actually writing fiction, the most important piece of equipment to a writer has is not his notebook but his memory. When writing a novel the work is ninety-nine per cent *remembering* because there is so much that cannot be checked as fact, and a good novelist must be able to close his eyes to recapture scenes exactly, in detail, and listen in silence so that he can recall exactly what people say. I have as a matter of fact almost total recall, and while it's never about anything important – though it must be important to me – I can meet people again after 10 years and can remember what was said on the previous meeting. Unless you have that faculty you have no business being a novelist.

A novelist thinks concretely, you would say? He enacts his themes out in terms of personal relationships, dilemmas?

Yes, a novelist has always to think in the concrete. Theorising is the death of the novel, it kills a story stone dead. And refusal to fill in properly also kills a novel; it isn't enough to sketch in background or descriptions of people or to ignore it altogether since the reader wants to know and has the right to know. The writer can't gloss over it. Sometimes the novelist will present the background in a short space, in a few words, but this won't work if you do that in few words. To quote Hemingway again, a good writer wanting to describe say, a nightclub must describe the interior in meticulous details, paint a picture, then chuck away all but about three square inches of that picture. As long as that tiny area is sufficiently done, then it is enough, but only if the whole has been done properly; it's no use to do *only* the three square inches. That's another aspect of the novelist's task, to know what to throw away – you have to throw a great deal away.

Is it exhausting to revise? Do you write a chapter and revise, or write a considerable portion of the novel and then revise?

I generally try to do the job in three drafts. The first draft as quickly as I can, then a second more detailed draft but still fairly rough, and then the final draft, straight through each time rather than revising chapter by chapter. Again and again you get hold of this lump of stone and first hew it into rough shape quickly, then include more detail, and finally and terribly carefully complete it, because if you make mistakes at that stage you can't rectify them; if you're incautious your subject may not have any nostrils – mind you in some sculpture I suppose that wouldn't matter, and in some types of novel it doesn't seem to matter, but I belong to a realistic school.

Can you say who your influences are? English novelists of the twentieth century?

Well firstly I won't say much about Tolstoy, Dostoevsky, Dickens, though Wells is there, the Wells of *Kipps* and *Mr Polly,* but simply to say they were an influence is not to make much of an impact because one would need to write a book about them to do them justice and explore in detail all that they have meant to me. In our own times I still have an enormous admiration for Thomas Wolfe who is today unjustly neglected and though I know he has many faults, almost insuperable faults, nevertheless he seems to me a great novelist, and the reason he is not accepted today is that he did things on too large a scale. Then one has admiration for Scott Fitzgerald although the volume of his achievement, his real achievement, is remarkably small because so much of his work was hack work, but that portion which was true and will last is better almost than anyone else's this century, so much so that you wonder why it's worth bothering to read anyone else's. And Dos Passos, that is the early Dos Passos before Dos Passos started making propaganda for Barry Goldwater, a good thing in itself – I'm all for it – but it seems to have had the worst possible effect on Dos Passos. I've put on record my admiration for Dos Passos in an article for the *New York Times.* I used to admire Salinger more than I do now, which is quite unfair since he is still the same writer he was, but when a lot of absolute morons began to praise him and got into the act I don't feel I want to look at him anymore; he is a very good writer with a really penetrating vision.

Of English novelists I think there's no doubt that our finest living novelist is Anthony Powell – they pronounce it 'Pole' but that's ridiculous because no one ever knows who you mean when you say that. I don't think any living novelist in England has his detachment, an almost architectural sense of construction: you can see the shape of his novels and sequences which are already becoming plain, awe-inspiring, an enormous job, in this 'Dance To The Music Of Time' series. And he writes the best English of any novelist now extant, there's no doubt of that. Although his range appears to be narrow, when you look at him properly his range is very wide, and it's a puzzle to me why more fuss is not made of him. Among poets, there are three to whom I always return: one is Rainer Maria

Rilke, the other is W.B. Yeats, and the third is John Betjeman who is badly underestimated because so many critics and reviewers are squalid, vulgar and petty without any real taste, and all of them long ago succumbed to the illusion that to be a good poet you must write epics about grand subjects whereas the mark of the true writer is what he knows about and what is close at hand. I would put it this way, that a real painter would never want to do something obvious like Mont Blanc but would be far more interested in an empty coffee cup, a bowl of fruit, something commonplace. A real artist will only be bothered to fall in love with a girl he can actually go to bed with; he doesn't dream about the unattainable when his appetite is so sharp and so lusty that he has to have a girl he can get hold of here and now. I mean that as a metaphor, of course.

I know this is usually hush-hush with a writer, but I imagine you are working on another novel, so can I ask if there is anything you would like to achieve in the future, something you haven't essayed so far? Or is that an unanswerable question until you are settling down to achieve it?

From now on each of my novels will be quite different, though as I said, the novels so far have been different. *Room At The Top* and *Life At The Top* were in sequel and are really one big novel and ought to be published together, but I try to do something different in each book and now the time has come to use different backgrounds and I don't want simply the same people in different surroundings; I want the works to be entirely different because if you don't keep on trying new things then you become sterile in the end, you don't get anywhere, though it is possible to keep turning out the kind of fiction that would enable you to make a living, and I want to do that as much as anyone else, but if I don't continue to enjoy writing – as far as anyone can be said to enjoy writing – then there's no point in me doing it. The new novel[2] will, I hope, give readers the same shock that the *Jealous God* gave them, although I can't predict that they will be as pleased by the shock as they were by the *Jealous God*.

-----◆•◆-----

[2] *The Crying Game* (1968)

Brigid Brophy (1975)

I came to know you initially not through your writings but through your reputation, your advocacy of Public Lending Right. But before we discuss that phase of your life perhaps we can talk about your literary work. When I began to read your novels I was struck by your classicism – I mean your Latin and Greek which is clearly there in the novels. Can I therefore begin by asking how much the Classics have meant to you and how much they have shaped your work?

You are a good detective. Yes, my background is classics; I was offered the opportunity to learn Greek when I was 13 and thought I would have a bash at it for six months or so. When I went up to Oxford I did read classics and this was because I wasn't previously allowed to learn Greek at school; I was anti-Latin, though I have come round to it a little since then. But my early, deep and abiding love is for the Greek language.

Does any particular author appeal to you?

Oh, Homer, the basic one – the equivalent of Shakespeare. And insofar as I can make anything of them at all, the poems of Sappho which are like a broken mosaic. Lucian, oddly enough. And in Plato something simple like the *Crito* or the *Apology,* which are completely accessible, and very moving and appealing; the death of Socrates is probably the only justifiable deliberate martyrdom.

Another thing that struck me as I read your fiction, The Snowball, Hackenfeller's Ape, *less so in* In Transit *(more of that later), and again in* The Adventures Of God In Search Of The Black Girl *was the approach to life through the exercise of reason. Now that itself is very Greek, isn't it? Or does that not matter – would you have been that kind of person anyway?*

I think one has to be reasonable; there is a simple compulsion to be reasonable, which may be a moral one, but it is there, and I think the Greeks were susceptible to that compulsion. One can't say to oneself deliberately, "I will be unreasonable, or rather, I will be anti-reasonable." One has to invent rationalisations, and if you wish to come to unreasonable conclusions then that would mean driving yourself mad; you have to create logical worlds. Otherwise you see the heavens opening in a vision and see someone coming down to offer a revelation. You have to go mad to be deliberately unreasonable, but of course the place where reason doesn't quite go the

33

whole way is in aesthetics; I think reason will go the whole way to show you what the pattern means in a work of art and you may also be able to pick on certain twirls and curves in the pattern and say those are what is the meaning, but the act of putting everything together and quite explaining the underlying meaning is beyond reason. It is unreasonable to be so ardent in the pursuit of beauty which isn't necessarily a reasonable method of behaviour; it might be better to settle for comfortable prettiness than for constantly searching for something that is beautiful, i.e. a masterpiece.

The definition of "beautiful" is very difficult. One might begin by establishing that things that are beautiful have certain qualities, order perhaps, or are satisfying in some way, but then the description of what is called "beautiful" can vary tremendously. Is this where you have to leave calculation and analysis and expose yourself to the object?

You certainly have to be wary of any generalisation because as you imply that is unsound, but I would say that any work of art is not beautiful to me unless it has a pattern. Certain romantic artists suggested quite the opposite, that if it has pattern it is second-rate, and they are not swept away by it unless it has no discernible pattern. One is in a world where one cannot lay down general rules, and reason is all about laying down general rules, and you could show me endlessly what is so good about a drawing and I would quite agree with you, and after lengthy analysis you might say, "This moves me" and I would reply, "It doesn't move me." At that point nothing can be done about it.

You were reported as saying that two of the themes in life which, if they do not obsess you at least interest you, are summed up in the Greek words "eros" and "thanatos," "love" and "death," very basic experiences. Do they summarise what you seek to pursue as themes?

I think it might be true of everybody. I was thinking of "eros" and "thanatos" not only in Greek terms but also in the psycho-analytical sense of Freud, who was a good Grecian in his way and named these two basic instincts. I have strong sympathy with psycho-analytical thought and have written a certain amount about it, so possibly when I said that I was thinking more in Freudian terms than in the Greek.

How do you think the psycho-analyst differs from someone like yourself, a writer of fiction, in seeking to understand the puzzlement of life, of existence, of relationships?

Only in that he doesn't write fictions! Many psycho-analysts, including Freud, have been very good writers, and I think there is too much snobbery about creative writing: writers are mainly responsible for it because they are not paid enough so they have to insist that they are creative, which means they can't pay the rent or buy next week's shopping. I don't think there is any great divorce between the sort of imagination that produces a work of art and the sort of imagination which produces a hypothesis, and most creative scientific thinking is the production of hypothesis, and a hypothesis is simply a fantasy, the basic material of scientific thinking just as fantasy is the basis of artistic thinking. Having generated fantasy both the scientist and the artist have to set to work to test it, and they test their fantasies by obviously different criteria; the scientist wants to know if his hypothesis, his particular fantasy, is compatible with the facts, and the artist wants to know if his piece of fantasy material can be made to work as a work of art. In a way the artist is more pragmatic, less generalised, more like a craftsman, and he will judge it a good fantasy if its patterns form a consistent structure like a building – all artists are like architects – and that is the test of that kind of fantasy. To the scientist the test is to ask if it fits in with the known facts, the discoverable facts, but the actual process, the production of the fantasy, is mentally, intellectually, and I think psychologically too, very similar, almost identical.

The making of life into a novel when thought about coldly is a strange form of activity, isn't it? Say, an account of walking along from here out into Old Brompton Road, catching a bus and going to the shops, then meeting a friend and having dinner with him tonight – turning that into a fictional experience is an odd practice. Does it strike you as such, or does it seem absolutely natural and necessary?

It does strike me as absolutely natural and necessary. But if it goes wrong it can leave one thinking what a strange thing to be doing! All is well as long as one has faith in a work, but one can lose that faith in it, lose one's willing suspension of disbelief for the moment, apparently by accident, though there is probably psychological reason for it, but it does happen, and then as you say one has a sudden sense that it is a curious thing to be engaged on. It is rather like those hot, thunderous summer afternoons as a child when one suddenly lost a sense of reality, even of the ordinary world, let alone the imagined world.

Is writing an exciting experience for you or is it strictly cerebral, perhaps like translating a book of Virgil into English?

Writing something of one's own is more exciting than translating someone else's; if you pause at line 37 of a book of Virgil it won't go away overnight, but in original writing there is always a dreadful fear that one won't write up one's notes quickly enough, or one's text quickly enough, a dreadful fear that the scene in the next but one chapter won't be able to be written before you reach it, that the marvellous scene will have vanished from memory.

Scenes may occur to you in any order and once engaged with the scene imaginatively you must get it down?

There are terrible dangers in getting it down. It may not fit; working in from two ends of the tunnel, it may not meet. Some writers whom I admire very much are capable of plotting the whole thing in advance, writing synopses then going back and beginning the writing; that way they must spare themselves an enormous amount of anxiety, of lying awake at night, reaching into the dark, trying not to wake one's husband to scribble something and in the morning being unable to decipher the scribble. But for me to write a synopsis would make it go dead, become an academic exercise. I have to be excited, but across the excitement is anxiety and sleeplessness.

Once the idea begins to grow in your mind can you live with it and disgorge it fairly quickly?

Yes. It can lie around for a long time, sometimes for years, but it's like blowing up a balloon – one can blow up and blow, then suddenly it starts to form and blows up big. I am quick at that but I think I'm getting less quick as I grow older, perhaps through grinding out so many memoranda on behalf of the arts!

I noticed in reading The Snow Ball, *which I imagine was a carefully constructed, convoluted piece of work, that the Mozart motive from* Don Giovanni *runs through it; Mozart crops up in several places in your work – is this evidence of a particular regard for that composer?*

Yes, I wrote a book called *Mozart The Dramatist*, about his operas, and he has been a matter of deep concern; my husband wrote a biography of him some years ago*, so my life does revolve around Mozart.

*The Life And Death Of Mozart (1971) by Michael Levey

36

Is he the musical equivalent of someone in literature who would display the same qualities and to that extent satisfy you?

I don't know that there is the precise equivalent in literature – one would like to say "Shakespeare" but Mozart is so classical and Shakespeare is so formless.

Pope or Dryden?

Yes, I admire both Pope and Dryden and indeed love them very dearly but neither had that melodic quality of Mozart, and there isn't quite that enormous vitality.

I did enjoy your Fifty Works Of Literature We Could Do Without *which prompts all sorts of suggestions for inclusion. I take it you meant it seriously, that it wasn't just a jeu d'esprit?*

No, it wasn't, and indeed the fact that it was taken as an attempt just to throw mud at some authors was itself interesting, and we three authors of it – myself, my husband Michael Levey and Charles Osborne – felt we had made our point. We took the view that those who don't *dis*like some works of art don't genuinely like *any* works of art. One meets enthusiastic old ladies, and most critics are enthusiastic old ladies (in the spiritual sense) prepared to gush at anything and are closely related to my mother who is convinced that all classical music is beautiful, consequently she never goes to concerts or listens to records or to the radio; in fact she doesn't like music. If you ask her about Mozart, Schubert, Beethoven – she will reply, "Oh, so lovely," and we came to the conclusion that people like that don't really like works of art at all. To put oneself to the test and ask which works of art were beautiful one finds some of them like magazine stories; my own favourite candidate as a magazine story in the book just mentioned is Wuthering Heights. It seems to me that that book if published now would be thought to be a work of a late follower of Daphne du Maurier.

Your mention of your mother reminds me of your other parent, your father, John Brophy, a novelist who began the move towards authors' rights with Brophy's Penny in 1950. Were you influenced by him to become a writer, or even in spite of him?

I think by the time I was grown-up it was rather in spite because we were very different sort of writers and I was always frightened of treading on his toes and he was frightened of treading on mine, and we were fond of each other but with very different tastes except that we were both inordinately fond of literature. We used to quarrel like mad over matters of taste; I think as a small child I thought everybody was a writer, that it was quite straightforward, that when one grew up one's galley proofs would come, and one would have a room of one's own which one was never required to dust – that this was what being grown-up meant. When things became clearer to me I think I was frightened of even saying I wanted to be a writer, because of him, and if asked at parties, "What do you do?" I would answer that I was a shorthand typist, not wishing to embarrass him either by being a much worse writer and so letting him down, or a much better writer and thereby hurting his feelings.

He was from Liverpool. Does that mean you were born in that city?

No; he came to London where I was born.

Just before leaving the subject of literature and its critics whom you describe as old ladies, there is one critic who is anything but like that and is so influential that anyone who has read English at all in the past forty years can't possibly have avoided him. You will know right away that I mean F.R. Leavis. What are your feelings about him?

Unmentionable on tape! I'm not without admiration for him; I just wish to God he wasn't such a poor writer. The actual muddy impasto he makes of the language makes me almost unable to read what he has written and so discover what his drift is though his drift may be highly sympathetic.

Now we have mentioned John Brophy who began the movement for authors' rights, perhaps one of the earliest if not the earliest pioneer, and you have spent a good many years as possibly the chief advocate of Public Lending Right. Can I ask how your interest arose and what is the state of play so far?

What my father suggested in 1951 was a mistake, and were he alive now he would readily agree it was a mistake – the idea of paying a penny to the author every time a book was borrowed. If you cast your mind back to that time you will remember that it was thought we had overcome poverty and that we would all be affluent and equal for evermore. We were not affluent but the statistics which showed we weren't were not generally available and I think my father felt that prewar poverty, depression had vanished. He persuaded the Society of Authors to take up the idea, and after much difficulty in persuading them to do so, eventually they did adopt it though they insisted from the the start that the publishers should take a share; whether or not that is still their official policy nobody quite knows. We don't ask about it in the hope that publishers won't dash in and take their cut.

Everybody thought that everything was going ahead fine, as I did; I was an inactive person in writers' circles, paying my subscriptions thinking the Society was there to look after professional writers' interests. My father died in 1965, and then suddenly in 1972 one realised that the Society of Authors had given their welcome to Lord Eccles's report on Public Lending Right. I read the report carefully and thought surely they aren't seriously suggesting that payments should not be related to loans of books from libraries, but there should be no payments on books already in libraries. It can't be that the Society genuinely welcomes this scheme because any writer now old who was not producing any more books would receive nothing under this scheme even though he might have a considerable *oeuvre* of perhaps twenty or so titles from his past still in the libraries and being borrowed. But it appeared that the Society at that stage did approve the Report. Several writers stood up and protested at a meeting of the Society– I was one – others were Francis King, Lettice Cooper, Maureen Duffy, and we were given a tough reception, the Society saying that in their view the scheme was better and that payment by loans wouldn't work, too bureaucratic. The five of us thereupon founded Writers' Action Group which began by asking people we knew to write to people they knew. Several writers gave us their signatures and then finance, and what we in fact did was to discover that the loan sampling scheme could work. Maureen Duffy is unfrightened by machinery and electronics, and I although no mathematician am unfrightened by statistics and find computers exciting.

We simply went round to various interested parties – we visited computer firms and makers of electronic machinery and discovered what we ought to have known though we weren't well enough educated in all this to realise, that various kinds of apparatus could easily be used to record loans, to work out what an entitlement is, and other data. After that technical discovery WAG flourished and we asked a friend if he could put us in touch with a statistician and came up with Ronnie Tuck of Bedford College who was charming and luckily fascinated by the problem of sampling and said he would love to draw us up a grid, that 72 public libraries would be enough.

This he did and WAG presented the results to the Government who continued to say it was nonsense; we then had a number of computer firms confirm in writing that it was not nonsense, at which the Government found computer firms whose findings were that the scheme would work! After which the Society of Authors changed its tune and is now supporting WAG and we are all good friends and much of the top brass of the society is now supporting WAG; we now get on better with the newer brass.

And how far now in 1975 do you think the battle has gone in your favour?

The government has taken this point, that it acknowledges that it will pay out of central funds, something that is vital to librarians and particularly vital to writers. So long as there are public libraries funded one way or another publicly, writers are dependent on them, and any attempt to cut their book funds would be disastrous, consequently although not all writers' organisations are very clear on policy as to where the money should come from, WAG has from the start asserted that it should come from central government funding. When we met St John Stevas – and this was very sweet of him, he said he might make it half central funding half from the rate support grant or half directly from local authorities – and he's never had such a lot of money before! However that came to nothing.

With the Labour Party we have never had any trouble about central funding since public libraries are a sacred trust of the Party – in fact the sacredness of the libraries was an obstacle to us in the earlier part of our campaign. However, their attitude did work in our favour because the new Minister Hugh Jenkins never wavered from the idea of central funding. The issue now is when? A few days ago I heard it would be November 1975 at the earliest. The other issue is which distribution scheme would be most efficient and despite some objections it looks as if the purchase scheme will be the accepted one. The purchase scheme means that a sum which is a proportion of the purchase price of the book be paid to the author, and authors also want to be paid in proportion to the loans of their books in libraries and they want to be paid annually because of course authors receive no regular monthly salary and the knowledge that even a small amount was available to them each year would be valuable to them, especially in old age since they do not qualify for pensions either; in fact they do not have an earnings related pension scheme because they are self-employed, and old age is a crucial time for many of writers who face destitution then, so that the purchase scheme can mean some security.

The Library Association concedes the justice of the cause but objects to the way and means of collection because it would be too expensive; instead it alludes to devices such as reductions of income tax for authors. How do you feel about their objections?

Many authors do not pay any income tax – I haven't paid any for three years. A recent survey showed that 56% of authors in the UK earn less than £500 a year by writing and they of course have to go out to work to keep going, so talk of tax concessions cuts no ice with us since we aren't in that sort of bracket. The actual administrative cost of loan sampling as established by the Department of Education and Science (not by us) is £285,000 a year, about half of which goes to pay the bureaucrats and librarians and local authorities, the other half is for the computer programming, and other necessary machinery, bar codes in the books etc. A little help from government in all this could reduce those costs ten percent or more.

You will have had much commerce with Hugh Barry, Secretary of the Library Association, during the past few years, crossing swords with him, you on behalf of the Writers' Action Group and he putting the opposite case on behalf of public libraries. What is your opinion of him? A worthy opponent, a man who finally saw the light?

At first of course he was the dragon, our relentless opponent in the struggle for Public Lending Right; then suddenly he summoned us in the Writers' Action Group to go and see him in his lair and we found him a charming, a consciously charming and witty Irishman playing on his Irish charm. When he found that WAG was insisting on central funding as the source of finance for a PLR and that libraries' book funds would not be affected, Hugh Barry relented, and we hoped that the whole of the Library Association had relented – in that we turned out to be wrong. Still, we retained very amusing and certainly happy memories of Hugh Barry himself.

Note: Public Lending Right was finally introduced in 1979.

A.S. Byatt (1976)

Antonia, can we take up this conversation from the place we left it earlier, before the tape recording, when you said to me that Iris Murdoch had told you that she felt you would have made a good philosopher had you not become a novelist? What do you think lay behind that observation? What was she saying about you?

I think she was saying that I am interested in the theoretical use of the language. I write letters to her about aesthetics and I need to think strongly about the aesthetic structure of anything I'm doing, particularly about people's use of language. But I'd make a bad philosopher in the sense that I would find it hard to hold, or think that anybody could hold, a belief about the nature of things. I'm interested in belief but it's basically a novelist's interest, and though I'm interested in language it is a sloppier interest than a philosopher would need to have.

You have to express your deepest vision, aperçus or whatever, in terms of fiction?

It's partly sensuality, though at the moment I find I write better when I'm writing abstract prose than when I'm writing fiction, but when I do that (the former) I'm not writing about the things I most care about. It isn't complete enough; it's a much more partial thing to do. I like to embody the abstract in the fiction but I wouldn't like only to write clear, lucid argument because so much would be missing of what it is that I know and one has a compulsion to convey everything one knows, something I fail to understand, but there it is.

This means that you prefer to write amply, to write yourself into a good many words?

Yes, a great many words and preferably a great many people, preferably people who are functioning on many levels. We were also talking about Robbe-Grillet this morning and I said that I had recognised in him this compulsion to collect physical objects. He seems to me to have constructed a theory which makes this the only truthful and ideal aim of the novelist, to record things literally *seen*. I wouldn't wish in any way to be so restricted; I like people in my books to be able to think clearly and lucidly but I also like to convey other states of being in which people don't think clearly and lucidly but do see objects. Now that seems to me to be the glory of the novel and I don't see why it should be thought a thing of the past. It can convey within a loose but structured framework a great many things at once, which is the kind of art I would like to do if I can do it.

At what point does "structure" enter your mind? Take your second novel, The Game. *At what point did that begin to take shape itself as it ended up: at an early stage, or do you work yourself into it by saying what you have to say in terms of character, letting your dialogue emerge? When do you begin to edit it into the final form?*

It is a very slow process with me. I get distressed because the middle is so unhappy. I started both the novels I've written with a clear narrative compulsion covering most of the plot: this story had to be told and in both cases the story had to be constructed out of two disparate experiences that I knew could be made to form parts of the same whole. I then floundered in both cases, for some years trying to see how to fit it, how to make it sharper, which it wouldn't become, including a deal of self-indulgent drama which had to be cut out. It's the point at which I begin to see what my framework of metaphors is that the whole thing starts tightening up and moving very fast, and often this is a surprising development out of the narrative.

I wrote a very bad draft of the first novel[1] and then wrote a pretty well complete, dead draft of the second, and then finished the first novel. Having seen where I was going with what I called the "undertow," that is, the unifying language and metaphors and the running ideas which connect my bits, and then I finished the second one. But I need these long gaps while I see what it was that I was really doing.

Do you have trouble about relating? I mean relating what you have to say – the events, the circumstances – are you concerned about having to fill so many pages "relating" in the old sense of the word and then worrying about how much space you should devote to that and when ought you to get into the exchange of words with your characters when you leave one kind or dimension – say, flashbacks, or the past – and when you want to hurry your characters, introduce them and involve your reader in a conversational way? Does that balance occur as a problem? Or is that a layman's view of the way a novelist works?

I thought I'd solved it because the last draft of the second novel went along very fast and I thought, "I know how to do this and I shall never have this trouble again." In fact I'm having this trouble again with every

[1]*Shadow Of A Sun* (1963)

chapter of the new novel now[2]. I think I have the collecting compulsion in me, a primitive instinct – I wish to live through each scene, therefore I have to write everything; I have to know how they got there, why they got there, who paid for it, how many times they have been in similar situations, what they remembered, what they all saw, what linguistic echoes struck them, and then I take almost all of that out again. This morning I reduced four pages to one side of narrative, and then it would go whizzing along. I then wrote another two pages very slowly and they will have to be reduced, to be adjusted.

Is this adjusting process unconscious or a very deliberate act?

It is quite deliberate. I suppose it's the creative bit; I feel immensely released when I have some sort of a text in front of me which can be cut down rather than a scene which I have to know completely and therefore has to be recorded completely in no matter how bad prose. I like to cast round, and if I know exactly where I'm going with any piece of writing too early then all sorts of things I might have discovered by this rather sloppy mode of approach get lost. Whereas if you put down everything you can think of in all directions around a scene of course it's unreadable, but let it lie for a week, you can see what were the essentials, some of them because they were well written and so stand out, and some because they link tightly and neatly to the rest of the book. I'm partly a very conscious writer and partly an instinctive writer.

Can you see the essentials because you are an instinctive writer, or is this the critic in you coming uppermost?

I do get clinical. It's a bit of both: it's rather like that thing E.M. Forster said which is a very true, about a large hill coming, and he was a more instinctive writer than I am although very ordered. You can tell when you are casting around for what will be a marvellous point, when you actually get there even though all you have is perhaps a colour flash or a slight geometrical or hint of where it is. You know it's lying there to be found.

Presumably you work to a routine, a method. Is it essential?

It is becoming essential because of the timescale I'm working on. I'm trying to write a very long book, a four volume novel, and I can only work

[2]*The Virgin In The Garden* (1978)

in shorter bursts than by nature I should need, so I keep myself going by keeping a complicated system of notebooks.

How does that work?

I keep a half a dozen thick notebooks on this novel and I tend to read purposefully for the novel. One of the themes is Queen Elizabeth I and I've read around her very carefully and collect little quotations. Then I jot down things I've thought of perhaps for the next three volumes, and I've taken to indexing the notebooks so that I know where to look up what I need. Because I've spent so many years on this there are layers of thought which I can't recall all at once when I come to needing them. And this does keep one going, provides continuity, because even if I can't get a free day to write a piece of novel it is easy to find half an hour in which to make a decent working note, and it's very important to keep the theme running in my mind. I often find the notes more spontaneous than the text because the first text is always bad anyway.

I have bought an index book and am indexing all my notes under the names of the characters and also under the big themes, which is interesting because I can see what they are going to be. One of the images I have is of burning, and the burning idea comes up at the end of volume 2 of the note books where there is a spate of notes on burning, that is, people burning. I started collecting poems. I still don't know why but I know it's important; though I don't know where it will be important I know which characters it applies to. But very often those things so carefully worked out don't ever get in at all and one has to have the courage to leave them out if they turn out not to be in it. I do have other notebooks and a commonplace book which is for snippets, and thoughts and occasional bursts of diary writing which only last about a week or so.

But your method for writing a critical work, for instance the work you are writing on George Eliot[3] at the moment, will this differ substantially from the method you have just described?

That is simply a card index of quotations, mostly from her and other people. Not including my own because I don't write anything down much until I start writing a book if it's criticism which I find I can write much faster and is much easier. Diaries I have kept for about nine months at a

[3]*George Eliot: Mill On The Floss* (1979)

time, usually only when I was miserable, so they are only one kind of diary. I have never re- read any of them. Some of the notebooks have analytic bits which are sources of novels not yet thought up. The commonplace book is mostly about Coleridge or Frank Kermode's criticism, or aesthetics, usually something philosophical. When the novel is really going I don't turn to the commonplace book, but only when I'm doing critical work – or just living, and then I take it on holiday with me. I tend to think more clearly then.

Does Iris Murdoch do this?

She says she doesn't. She says she works everything out entirely in her head, that she has a complete image of a novel in her head before she starts writing it. All the scenes are planned, the form is planned, and she cannot then deviate from this planned form even if she wants to because she complains they aren't spontaneous.

What is her gestation period – does she spent several months having something forming in her head which she then writes in two or three months?

I don't know how long ahead she thinks about a novel. I always have one in my head besides the one I'm writing, and even one or more of the four vaguely simmering.

Are you influenced in your critical work by contemporary authorities or do you prefer to shut them out?

I prefer to shut them out because my critical work I see as useful in working out how to write a good novel, and I'd rather learn from the source of whatever I'm writing on; it's better for me if I work it out for myself.

Is the texture of your writing changing over the years?

I'm behind with it, and that's a very big problem at present. It isn't changing because I haven't had enough time to write, to evolve the style. I've evolved the thought, the plot has changed, the form of the novel I'm writing because of the notebooks moving, and indeed the style of the notebooks is clearer, sharper and more complicated than in the first two novels. The actual prose I'm writing in the present novel is too full of sensibility, which irritates me, and I don't know how to undo it except by doing it like that and then looking at it, seeing what's wrong with it, than in trying to write it in another style. I can't start writing in another style yet. I haven't got an available prose to write the kind of thing I want to say.

Are you unconsciously affected by previous writers? Will this style which you may wish to change be affected by someone who impressed you, say Emily Bronte today or George Eliot herself?

If they do affect me I've forgotten, but if I forget something which did affect me deeply it echoes itself – and there's always a time lag before I recognise it. In *Shadow Of A Sun*, the first novel, I used a sentence straight from *Lady Chatterley's Lover*, the bit about forestry and trees being torn up, and it took me until I was teaching *Lady Chatterley* to realise I had done that. In the first two novels I didn't know that I was echoing Tennyson's *Morte d'Arthur* at times of crisis but I clearly was, the actual movement of the words; I don't know that anyone would have picked it up but I know where the rhythms came from. Now that I know I do that, I think it's unlikely to be *Morte d'Arthur* at crisis point in any future novel. Proust, too, I know I echo, I can't help, and that was quite a good thing to be troubled by.

You don't see the novel as a sermon, do you?

Not at all, no. I see it much more as an object, as a painting.

You would think it fatal to see it as a speaking to others, in an urgent or evangelical way – to your unseen readership?

Yes it would be, partly because the only thing I would want to say in a sermon would be, "Beware people who preach sermons" and "Beware people with strong beliefs, and people who tell you that!" No, this is very Bloomsbury and more post-Bloomsbury, in fact an Angus Wilson ethic, I think I have, but things are never what they seem, whereas some things must be what they seem, in fact.

Thinking about your audience – do you have any idea who your audience is,? Do you address any particular kind of person?

No. Partly because the writing I most like is always a person talking to himself. The things that move me personally most as writing are Coleridge's Notebooks, which is private, and Proust who is probably the most private novelist; in a sense you have to be Proust. Nobody can *receive* Proust, you have to be with him and go through it with him. Henry James, too. And among critics, Frank Kermode who is also talking to himself much of the time.

All novels are a private dialogue, so would it matter if yours weren't published?

It wouldn't stop me, partly because in the end there will come along someone who will see what one was doing – every novelist is sustained by that – and partly because it's nice to live with a theorem, the ability to say anything complicated or anything deep, a word I don't like using. That must take time, and it must take time for anyone to read it, which isn't that I've said anything yet, but the intention is there.

Would you be interested in creating a novel with a memorable hero or heroine? Or is that irrelevant to you – a Molly Bloom or a Leopold Bloom sticking out of it?

I think if one did it, it would be by accident. There is a trouble in the novel at the moment, and one of the troubles one can see as a literary historian is that authors are not creating memorable people, that the novelist has shifted his interest from the outstanding individual. Samuel Beckett has no individuals; he's flattening them. Anyone who is writing good prose is not creating Leopold Blooms now.

Not even Iris Murdoch?

Her prose is not all that good because it harks back to a narrative form which was created in a society with different preoccupations. Frank Kermode said of her unkindly that she had settled into bourgeois Oxford.

One can't recall any striking characters from her – or anyone else today.

Significantly I did a broadcast with her and I said something about the poor lady who was weeping because everyone thought her just ordinary and self-satisfied – it was a character in one of her novels – and Iris said, "Oh yes, that one, now what was her name? Where did she come?" I don't think George Eliot would ever have said that about any character she had invented. They were all carefully created, sacrosanct people who couldn't be interchangeable. And Iris cares a great deal about the human individual and presents one's own interest in the human individual so one has to keep constantly rethinking it, but she doesn't make individuals like Bloom or like George Eliot's people.

Is that a loss?

I do feel it is a loss. I should like to be able to make somebody; though it's interesting you should have said that I never think of it as a primary aim.

Is there a serious readership somewhere for the serious novelist, or has it disappeared? Is there an artist and a public? In a relationship?

I think there is an artist and there is a public, complicated by the contemporary belief that everything is evanescent and by the increasing number of artists, which makes a difference. There are very few people willing to be the public of an artist; they are all artists in embryo because the ones who do the reading have been through a literature course which tells them the highest thing is to create, and we are getting a kind of art which says that the reader is a kind of creator, and so they create unfinished puzzles that the reader can finish for himself and feel that he is doing the work. As a reader I'm more humble than that. I prefer to see a complicated, a really finished piece of work that I couldn't have done and which I work on as a reader, not a creator. And as a writer I want to finish something, to do all the work I can do and not hoodwink or push around the reader. But there is an uneasy relationship with the reader. I think it has something to do with the kind of aesthetic education that everyone has had a bit of who reads at all. It is to do with our sense of culture, our sense of crisis, cultural crisis I suppose it's called, which I think has always been present and always being said not to have been the case before.

When you have produced what you have to say to your satisfaction do you see yourself as also judging what it is you have created? Are you both controlling and judging the subject matter, for example of your tetralogy, the novels you are working on now? Are the two words ones you could use without blushing?

I think so, though I never have finished anything in that sense yet. I have made efforts to see what sort of thing I could do; I wouldn't put it higher than that. I think to say that one controls and one judges is not to say that one is the final authority or that one view is the only view. There is a very necessary process of separating what one has lived through and worked through, which is a different matter, so that it can be contemplated not only by yourself but by other people, and what they bring to it will obviously be different and what they judge of it will obviously be different, but one is also offering a form of judgment. To write a book changes one a great deal: it changes what one sees, it changes one in little ways because you go about the streets and everything is interesting because it fits or it might fit or because in going through the streets you are an observer. I've been thinking of this since reading Robbe-Grillet – the extraordinary activity involved in converting things into language. That I should sit on a bus between 17 Earlsfield Road and the London Library and try to convert hundreds of different faces and other objects into words and patterns seems an odd thing to be doing. And just at that primitive level one is constantly arranging and judging, and then at the other end there are six notebooks talking about what little I know about education – obviously it changes me. It makes it hard to teach books if I'm not working because the primary feeling becomes a great hole, an emptiness.

And the crucial question: what kind of interaction is there between your own life, relationships, day-to-day living and what you write? This is something that is constantly appealed to in works of criticism, invoked as one of the most important reasons for reading novels, to share a vision of life, to enter into the context the creative artist offers. Is there a closely bound, interwoven relationship between what you write and how you live.?

There are so many relationships between what you write and how you live. I used to know a man who wrote novels and saying, "I will justify my life. I will justify my life. I will write a good novel." It seems to me statistically there is no *a priori* urgency to justify one's life by writing a good novel; one can justify one's life by living one's life! One's life is a separate thing and I would feel ashamed to think one's life was only important vis-à-vis a book. It is possible to live a life *and* write a book. You can't live the life and write the book in two separate categories because everything that goes into the book is of yourself and to pretend that it isn't is a lie. It's just that it mustn't be yourself at a very simple level. You mustn't be very simply crying out for attention or justifying your behaviour or consoling yourself with what you haven't got, or embellishing what you have got.

There is the other instinct which people don't seem interested in: when I read books as a girl I read them in order to see something I hadn't got. To read, say, *Middlemarch* is to offer you literally experience which you haven't had, and it is possible to write in order to create a hypothesis and to experience things you haven't experienced and not only to justify, describe or share what you have experienced. I don't know why serious contemporary writers at the moment go on and on about truth and honesty as though fiction in the old sense is something immoral. It isn't. Invention is a great human virtue.

G.S. Fraser (1965)

A conversation with G.S. Fraser, poet, critic, author of The Modern Writer And His World *and for a good many years a literary journalist. When did you leave writing for a living to take up academic work? You are now lecturing in the English department at Leicester University.*

Difficult to fix a precise date, but I came to Leicester when I was just over forty, in 1959, and in 1950–51 I had done about eighteen months teaching in Japan. During my days in journalism I did a great deal of evening lecturing at Morley College in London, so this job was not new but is the first continuous teaching post I've held in a university on the permanent staff.

Did you find a different sort of satisfaction in this work as compared with writing?

Yes. As you may know the tutorial system is still practised here, taking students two by two, which is more important than the lecture that I was used to, and that in a tutorial one can analyse a piece of literature or a poem in much more depth with just two students. In this way one can make a more solid judgment of it than in writing say four of five reviews or preparing a broadcast or lecturing to a large mixed audience, when one's tempted to shine or to cover a lot more ground.

When you had taken your degree did you decide to launch into writing?

That was a long time ago – in 1937 when the war was coming on, and I was in St Andrews in Scotland and like many Scotsmen with literary ambitions I was torn between schoolteaching, safe and dull, and journalism which is not literature; finally I joined the Aberdeen paper, *Aberdeen Press And Journal* as a sub-editor, then a reporter and feature writer until 1939 when I joined up on the outbreak of war.

You did contribute to Penguin New Writing?

In 1949. A long article on diction in English verse* commissioned by John Lehmann, and that's interesting because in the article I foretold the reaction against Dylan Thomas and the New Romantics, saying that we

*‘Some Notes On Poetic Diction’ (Issue 37)

were in for a period of more strict, more prosy poetry, the poetry of statement rather than imagery, and a few years later poets like John Wain and Elizabeth Jennings, the people called the Movement, arrived, and so it all proved true! Philip Larkin was among them, and I remember meeting some of them when they were still undergraduates at Oxford because I used to go there fairly regularly to the Poetry Society or the Critical Society and I saw all the little pamphlets, the Fantasy Press in which they appeared before they became famous, and some of them were in an anthology I got out in 1954 called *Springtime* with other poets of another sort, young people under thirty, which critics like Philip Toynbee said were a series of dull, flat poems and which a few years later were all the rage.

Is contemporary poetry your primary interest?

It's what I've written most about and what I find it easiest to write about. I find it difficult to write about or even lecture about, novels, because of course they are long and complicated so that it's hard to hold the whole plot in one's head, hard to know what to concentrate on, whereas a short poem is there in front of you, you can read it many times until you know it backwards and forwards, you can read it aloud and reading it aloud can do half your teaching for you, bring out the meaning.

Your book The Modern Writer And His World *must have made quite an impact on young students when it came out in 1953?*'

The very first edition was a book I wrote while while I was in Japan, for Japanese students. There's a long tradition of teaching English in Japan, often by poets: Edmund Blunden, Lawrence Binyon, D.J. Enright. After the war they were cut off from English literature, then I was given the job by the Foreign Office to bring them up to date, and one of the things I did was to write that book which is still popular in Japan and has been translated into Japanese, and it was only some years later in England when I was free-lancing and very short of money and I thought there must be many people in England who could do with a textbook of this kind. I sent the MS round to various publishers and it was Derek Verschoyle who did it and the firm collapsed almost as soon as he published it, but it was taken up by another publisher, André Deutsch, and went into three impressions and I notice that in public libraries it is taken out regularly, about once a week.

There is a lack of good introductions to the modern period, isn't there, a surprising lack?

A very surprising lack. It is a large and varied period and nobody can hope to be master of all of it, and I think partly my journalistic training and not being severely academic when I wrote the book I didn't realise how thorough you had to be, with lengthy bibliographies appended; I wouldn't have the courage to embark on it now!

A leading article in the Times Literary Supplement *of November 1964 was about this very question, the teaching of English in universities, to which you replied and which subsequently stirred up a controversy. One passage reads, "A fashionable phrase today is 'to be with it' and the departments of English are increasingly 'with it' with a vengeance. The reasons for this movement are not far to seek: the first is to the credit of English departments since they have realised that the eclipse of the classics was due to its teachers' failure to take advantage of the wonders of the literature. English teachers are sharply aware of the warning and in order to keep in touch with the latest generation which they are no closer than anyone else to understanding, they attempt to enlist their sympathies by introducing into the courses work which their students ought to feel as part of the living tissue of the age. The intention may be well but the effects are unfortunate." What do you feel about that kind of attack?*

I just wondered if the writer, whoever it was, had actually done any teaching of modern literature in a university or had had much experience of it, because in point of fact 'modern literature' is a misnomer as a university subject, or at least it can be misleading. I tried to make clear in my letter to the *TLS* that what 'modern literature' means is that there is a kind of change about the year 1880 with the early novels of Henry James, when people like Tennyson and Browning are growing old or dying and the new poets of the Nineties are beginning, the influences on Yeats, and a poet like Hopkins – there is a total change of mood, more introspective, more self-conscious, more conscious of literary form and the possibility of experimenting, and all this makes a unity, the sense of new possibilities, of uprootedness and even of isolation in life, and it runs through in a unified way. I would say that, far from being 'with it,' in a sense it is at an end. I don't think there has been any deeply experimental poetry in England (not America) since the *Four Quartets* of the early 1940s; that was the last great modern poem. I don't think we're living in the modern period in that sense but we're living in a contemporary period which we can't yet name, much of which is traditional in fiction, narrative poetry and verse. If I were teaching this period I would end it in about 1940, which is historical to young students who haven't a deep sense of history, and the T.S. Eliot of *The Waste Land* is quite as far away from them as Dickens; one has to put in just as much background information.

To quote another piece from the same article: "Teachers are encouraging the study of contemporary letters because these are studies they themselves want to pursue and by giving their courses this emphasis they may enjoy the pleasures of a complementary career."

I suppose what he means by 'contemporary' is the fiction of Iris Murdoch, Kingsley Amis or William Burroughs' *Naked Lunch*. But these are *not* taught – sometimes at the end of the summer term when the course is over you might amuse yourself and your children by talking about recent stuff which they and you might have read, but it is really at the end of a tough and complicated period when much very difficult writing was produced.

It is true, isn't it, but in the past few years there has been emphasis on the discipline of letters, making the students grapple with the texts and analysing and understanding quite rigorously in a way which was unknown previously? English used to be a cosy hour with your favourite master.

Yes, when I was at school in Scotland it was rather old-fashioned. At St Andrews University we were taught by George Saintsbury's son-in-law who had himself studied under Saintsbury so that we had literary history rather than literature: we had to know about Tottel's *Miscellany* and it didn't matter if you had never actually opened it. Dates and titles were plentiful but no real textual criticism, so that it was mainly memory work and if you were interested in the texts then you had to go to the library and get it up for yourself, decide what the literature was really like! But if discipline means looking closely at a text to prove that you understand it then I'm all for it, but I would say that the study of modern literature requires this. You can't 'do' *The Waste Land* without a sense of the meaning of 'civilisation' in the past, and the distress and confusion of our time or the sense of a generation that has actually gone. So we take them through this and try to see that they get the message, that they had read it and understand it.

Does it seem to you that English is taking over some of the functions of the classical languages and literatures, Latin and Greek?

Yes, though in some ways I am sorry that they are in decline because one of the effects of such decline is that even third year students misspell words with Latin roots since they have no analytical idea of the roots of words like 'comprehension' and 'apprehension' and their syntax has a sloppiness, a kind of disconnection which is not the case with those who have had a grounding in Latin prose. I never learnt Greek, but Latin is a very good discipline for writing English prose clearly and for having some sense of resonance. On the other hand, great as Latin literature is, English literature obviously has an enormously richer range and variety and greater human interest when students can get properly involved in it. The elements that have to be right, like tidiness and rhetorical structure, means that Latin helps one not only to read adequately but also to write.

Which leads neatly to the question – do you see any point at all in substituting Old English philology in place of Latin syntax in English courses?

I'm sure it has an intrinsic interest in itself – I found a study of Old English poetry rewarding, but I must say that it was no help for the study of contemporary grammar; both it and the ancient Scandinavian languages were simply like foreign languages.

The question of textual rigour inevitably suggests the grim shadow of Dr Leavis. What do you think of his work – do you think he has completed it now?

He's been offered a professorship at York and this has led to a new lease of life. I have in many ways a great admiration for him and many say that he is a bad stylist but a great teacher or an uneven critic but a major influence, but I would say the opposite. I have met too many people who have been taught by him, especially the younger ones, not those of the older generation like John Speirs or L.C. Knights who are fine independent critics in their own right, but people like David Holbrook who are always going on about 'maturity,' repeating the words of the master, more or less, and I think yes, teach people how to judge but for God's sake set them free and let them go on their own path, free to disagree with you. Some of Leavis's criticism is strikingly memorable, even things with which one finally disagrees, like the piece on Milton in *Revaluation* or the essay on Swift in *The Common Pursuit,* both incisive points of view and great criticism. And then in the *Lady Chatterley* trial I thought he had courage to assert that no, this was not a very good novel because there was too much animus in it, that Lawrence had let his feelings get in the way of writing a proper novel – and that criticism was in the face of the case made in the trial which verged on humbug, making it a holy book which ought to be included as part of the Anglican marriage service almost! That showed originality, and also of course that he wasn't going to follow any line, even if too many people started following what they imagined was *his* line; if too many people agree with what he said he will sharply disagree.

Do you think the word 'creative' can be applied to criticism as it is to pure literature?

This is tricky. I think criticism is a branch of literature and should be written with eloquence and wit, a sort of human warmth as some American critics like Edmund Wilson do. Too many British academic critics write just slab after slab of utility prose, deliberately, not allowing themselves to become funny or personal or at ease, and that is dreary. And of course many poets and prose writers have been fine critics: Johnson, Dryden, Wordsworth and Arnold, and Eliot too; Henry James on the novel, and indeed Lawrence on the novel were as creative when they spent some of their energies on criticism.

If you were about to tackle a course on say, The Novel in the Twentieth Century, which novelists would you pinpoint to study?

This year I'm doing such a course, and have spent five lectures on Henry James and several on Conrad who is very important, a political novelist bringing in issues of the day as *Nostromo* which deals with colonialism, clash of races, civil war, the conflict of an old effete civilisation and the barbarous forces beneath it. He's got it all and he has an attitude to life which is corrosive but not in the least self-defeating or mystical; of the novelists of this century he is the one with whom I feel most affinity. And D.H. Lawrence is of course important; I found as a Scot that at first he put my teeth on edge, but having lived for the past six years in the Midlands, I'm getting round to him. There are women novelists, like Virginia Woolf, Elizabeth Bowen, and Penelope Mortimer, and there are other minor writers one would need to consider. American novelists would be needed, though...

Norman Mailer?

He does what so many American novelists do, spreads himself about too thin in too many pages, though *The Naked And The Dead* had a big scale and a large intention, but there is too often too many pages for the amount of talk and action. *The Deer Park*, about Hollywood, was interesting. A lot of 'think' writing has come out of America, essays on the importance of being violent and uncivilised, rather thin and a substitute for the genuine creative act of getting down to the genre itself.

When you are making a poem of your own do you need a long time?

I lead such a busy life that with luck I can write perhaps two or two and a half poems a year, not always intending to write but occasionally I'm asked to write something. I've had in progress one on President Kennedy since I was in America when he was assassinated, and it was as if it had to come, an intuition, and I sat down at a typewriter; a rough draft came to mind which you work at from there until you feel you have it fairly right and send it away to a magazine and hope it is all right. I have it here. I was in New York State and saw it on television as most people did, so that it is made up of TV images, I suppose, and the general feeling of the weather at the time, the feel of the American winter, when the sun is very bright, and I tried to tie that up with the sense of greyness within. That poem was done after the *New York Review of Books* had asked me to send a poem soon after it happened, but the poem wasn't any good at all. Then came the Kennedy thing and all sorts of images came into my head, the main technical problem was to get the lines broken so that it reads like a slow march and with the proper rhythm…

Did the rhythm determine itself?

The rhythm did determine itself once I'd decided that kind was the thing to aim for, and the stanza about Mrs Kennedy standing by the pillars with the two little children – that was what Robert Graves would call a 'mood' stanza and that came all by itself – the rest I had to work on to fit.

There are some good individual lines: 'Apollo of the picture page.'

Several American friends have worried about that one which they thought brutal, and also the '*Life-Time* smile,' but it indicates that here was a public figure to some degree created by publicity and then suddenly the killing blows through the picture page and he becomes like a figure from Greek tragedy or a sacrificial king.

INSTEAD OF AN ELEGY

Bullets blot out the *Life-Time* smile,
Apollo of the picture page,
Blunt-faced young lion
    Caught by vile
Death in an everlasting cage,

And no more young men in the world,
The old men troop to honour him.
The drums beat glum
    Slight snow is swirled
In dazzling sun, pale requiem.

And pale dark-veiled Persephone,
A golden child in either hand
Stands by white pillars:
    Silently
It seems forever she might stand.

In bright grey sun, processionals
Of pomp and honour and of grief
Crown that dead head
    With coronals.
Some stony hearts feel some relief.

But not your heart, America,
Beating so slow and sure and strong,
Stricken in his
    Triumphal car.
Guard Caesar's bitter laurels long.

With soldier's music, rites of war
He had proved bravely when put on.
The soldiers shoot,
    Rage echoes far
Above the grave at Arlington.

Brian Glanville (1980)

Brian Glanville is equally celebrated as a sports writer, at present on the staff of the Sunday Times, and as a novelist, so we will try to tackle both these occupations. When we say 'sport' we think in your case of football, and indeed your first book was Cliff Bastin Remembers, published when you were 19 in 1950. He was one of the titans of his day, wasn't he?

He was, and I was very lucky at the time. If you look at my career it may seem to have been brilliantly planned when in fact it wasn't at all but simply happened in a most haphazard way. The Bastin book did turn out to be useful for me but it came about simply because I was an Arsenal fan. I felt personally grieved when he finished, and though I at 17 had never seen Bastin play at his peak, which was years before, I did see him play 32 times, but by then his pace had gone. I used to drive past the Cliff Bastin Cafe on the bypass at Edgeware and eventually I wrote to him suggesting he write a book with me which we did complete. He had retired in 1946, this was 1949, and if I had had any real knowledge of sporting journalism then I would have thought, 'Bastin has had his day, there's no market for a has-been,' but being just a fan and a hero-worshipper, such mundane considerations didn't enter into it, so the book was written. When it came out it had a *succès de scandale;* he was very frank and a certain process of osmosis had taken place, his feelings were my feelings and his thoughts were my thoughts, and I was surprised when a lot of people were upset, others said how cheeky he was, but I think he was honest, and being afflicted by deafness he tended to live in his own world. When the book came out it attracted a great deal of attention and did a great deal for me, though that was not my object in writing it.

Were you beginning to write sporting material for newspapers by then?

Yes, as soon as I left school I began writing for sports magazines, at the age 17 or so, and I was quite lucky. The first article I ever tried to write on football was in an ephemeral magazine, a monthly, published in Fleet Street, and I'm endlessly grateful to it. It was called *Sport* and later I was on its staff, after which it became *Sport Express* run by two sharp characters who changed the name to that because they found out the *Daily Express* was planning a Sport Edition so they thought they would like to be bought out. In its day it had prestige and launched many writers including the lawyer, Louis Blom Cooper QC, who always appears to be in the news; he wrote under the pseudonym Lou Cullis, his first journalistic series on amateur football for the *Sport Express* under my aegis!

By the time we reach the late 1950s you had had much experience of this kind of writing, and had begun to publish novels because your first novel, The Reluctant Dictator, *was in 1952.*

I wrote that when I was eighteen and it wasn't very good but it meant it was publishable and so helped me escape from study of the law in which I had been entombed for a spell. The fact of publication gives one incentive and encouragement to embark on a gamble like a career in authorship.

Did you make a clear distinction, once launched as a professional, between the writing of sports books and journalism and the writing of fiction?

Yes I did. I kept them apart though that first novel, a kind of satirical fantasy, was based on an actual occurrence in football. I realised early on that it was not possible to rely on a living out of fiction, though it's possible to be lucky, write one book and never have to write another, as some contemporary novelists have done. I knew fiction would need to be subsidised from my other output and in that I could be my own master; I wouldn't need to write potboilers for money. So in the event I have sometimes made a good deal of money out of a novel or short story and sometimes very little, but it never mattered.

On the other hand one was always being warned by friends about the dangers of journalism, and one recalled the fate of Cyril Connolly or read the words of Somerset Maugham. I think there are dangers but they seem to me to lie outside the realms of sports journalism because no matter how passionately one is interested in football – and I am still, in a totally adolescent way – it doesn't really impinge. What is difficult and dangerous is in that great area where you are dealing with something which can be easily handled in fictional terms and are tempted to deal with it in a journalistic way. To me, journalism means writing in a blinkered way, for various reasons, not always deplorable ones. Often, if I am writing about somebody I have interviewed, I will notice something about his speech or appearance, and in a novel or play that would all be part of a character drawing, but it can't be used in a newspaper piece in that way. It might hurt the person, and it would be too elaborate.

You must know that much sporting journalism is poor. Are you seeking to introduce higher standards into the craft – not in a prissy way, but aware that something has to be done?

Not really. I don't believe I initiated good standards of football reporting. Others have remarked that I brought better quality writing to football journalism but I repudiate that because it had been done before by, for example, Geoffrey Green from whom we all learnt a lot in the 1950s, and Don Davies the old international, and going back to the early years of this century, Jimmy Catton the greatest of all football journalists – he was a seer, a prophet as far as football is concerned and got everything right *and* set high standards. Although for better or worse my journalism might influence people, I think it is just the historical process: things were changing for historical and sociological reasons and I just happened to be there at the time. One might make a small contribution but *sub specie aeternitatis* I don't believe I make much difference to it at all.

Did you perhaps see that in your views, post Second World War, there was something fresh that wasn't there in pre-war football?

Only in one way – and then again there were people around who had done it as well or better than I had, and again whom I was able to approach and get help from. That was the relationship between British and foreign football. The book I wrote in 1955 called *Soccer Nemesis* was originally called *British Soccer And The Foreign Challenge*, the MS of which I scrapped and rewrote with the help of people like Dr Willy Meisl, a refugee from Austria who wrote high quality sports journalism and had written a book about the Austrian wonder team of the 1920s and 1930s. He was a famous continental journalist and a great help to me though he couldn't write English to save his life. He predicted total football in his book *Soccer Evolution* which came out the same time as mine. In Italy there was the manager of their international team for twenty years who later turned to journalism very successfully; he was my guru. I met him first when I was nineteen and when I went to live in Italy in the Fifties I made a great pilgrimage to his home. I had little money and couldn't afford a hotel so travelled overnight from Florence to Turin in a third-class carriage with wooden seats while Sicilians all round me were eating cheese. I spent a fascinating day with Vittorio Pozzo.

Your title Soccer Nemesis *was presumably prompted by England's awful defeat by Hungary in 1953? Was it then that you felt England had to recognise there was a big Europe out there with superior players?*

I knew already what was happening. I had been writing the book and planned the title before that game ever took place; I was well aware of the situation. I think if there was anything I brought to sports journalism, apart from perhaps the ability to write better than other reporters, it was the awareness, as you say, of what was happening out there.

And as a creative writer did you also have an inwardness to the personalities of footballers? Did that always mean something to you?

Yes indeed, that had always meant a lot to me. It's extraordinary but people who work in sports television often come up to me and say, "How can you bear to be in touch with such fellows, professional footballers? Don't they make you sick?" I must say I don't think I like today's generation of professionals as much as I like a lot of the older ones. They are somewhere out in No Man's Land, with upper middle class incomes and working class origins which they tend to lose touch with, but because they have not been brought up in a middle class environment, they can't adapt to one and therefore are out in limbo, what the *New Statesman* once called Nowhere People, the kind who turn up in roadhouses from out of nowhere and go off into nowhere, like the stupid, flashy ones who have made their money somehow (better not to inquire how).

Nevertheless I still like footballers on the whole; it is unfair to condemn them as stupid because I have some insight into their circumstances. For instance, my younger boy was taken on when he was 17 by a Third Division Italian club and lived there in Forli. He was thrilled by it all but after about a month he was caught up in the rhythm of the life and couldn't do a hand's turn! He was by then screaming to come back and get down to some school work! Now if someone like him from an academic background with two siblings at Oxford can't settle down to work in that atmosphere, what chance have kids who have thought of nothing but football from the age of eleven, with the kindly help of a club?

Why is Association Football so relentlessly working-class? It is now and always has been even though the players are lifted by money out of that class.

It wasn't always working-class. It had begun in the public schools, then in the 1880s there was the phenomenon of The Corinthians, and in about

1892 the whole England team consisted of Corinthians and they held their own with the professionals right up until the beginning of the First World War and it gradually slithered away as there was more intensive training. Nowadays few men from middle class families become professional footballers because the tendency is to believe the myth that unless you become a pro at 16 and leave school you haven't a chance.

Steve Heighway is an exception.

Yes, he is, and plays brilliantly for Liverpool and Ireland, is a graduate with 2nd class honours in economics from Warwick University. But middle-class families do not want to allow their children to commit themselves to that course, and also as in other spheres few are chosen though many are called; for every player who makes it even to Third Division level there must be fifty or a hundred who never make it at all.

And the image of the typical League football ground is of mean streets around it, and what J.B. Priestley described as 'the grey-green tide of cloth caps.'

Quite. But it isn't so abroad, though it is still true that few graduates play in Italy, Spain, South America.

And it is the question of starting young which discourages middle class families who have other ambitions for their children?

Yes, and in the same way there were never any Jewish footballers from the East End but there were lots of Jewish boxers, because they came from very poor families and if they were good with their fists they could make money quickly; there wasn't the money in football then, and if there had been, there would have been more Jewish footballers!

When you interview footballers for copy how do you cope with their relative lack of articulateness, or are they more fluent nowadays?

No – they always have been on the subject of their own game. There are some who can't say anything, but then that is so in any walk of life, actors, even writers can be inarticulate. Footballers are articulate about football, some marvellously so, as are many boxers about their world which is a much more chromatic and in some ways more sinister world. It's an individual matter and I don't think the present generation are as much fun or as lively and original as the players just after the war, though they can be shrewd about their game. The older players were remnants of that working-class, unreconstructed culture who were not affected by middle class morality and were very much their own men. They were more rounded people with a much clearer idea of who they were and where they stood, and while I wouldn't bring back poverty and the Jarrow march I did know many of these men and they were more four-square without that spiv-like quality of the modern footballer.

And what about the game itself? Rugby Union is an extremely complex, subtle game not only physically and visually but theoretically. Football seems simpler, more primitive – is that a fair statement?

Oh, it's an enormously complex game. What I love about football is that at one level it seems simple to understand, and indeed it is so, but on another level it is complex, and tactically it is a far more subtle game than rugby. There have been two or three tactical revolutions since the war, and there are so many different ways of playing it: the breakaway from the third back game of the Brazilians, the four-two-four, then the Germans and the Dutch bringing in 'total football' so-called, and the Italians with *catanaccio* and the sweeper defence. The longer I go on, the more there seems to be to find out about it; just understanding a game is very difficult.

A whole new language has emerged: 'sweepers,' 'strikers,' 'laying off the ball' and 'nutmegs'; words that in previous years did not exist.

It's coaching and courses, jargon that makes it easier to sound important. Much of the time the only effect is a complete inability to communicate with the players who are mostly instinctive anyway. I remember talking to John Arlott, telling me he was talking to Walter Winterbottom about the ability of certain players to see what was happening all round them, and Walter said, "Yes, we know about that and we call it 'environmental awareness.'"

Could you name the three best players since the war?

Pele, di Steffano and Best. And Maradona, coming up.

And two other British players?

Tom Finney and Stanley Matthews. Others come to mind but not perhaps of that quality; Finney was a very great player, and so was Tommy Lawton, by any standards. I don't think anyone in the 1966 World Cup team was of that calibre, not even Bobby Charlton.

Best came and went rather quickly, didn't he?

He was self-destructive. I liked him and got on with him well, as well as admiring his abilities, but he was a disturbed boy and you are never going to get that sort of comprehension at football club level; what do football managers know about psychology? There was at last some enlightenment when Wolverhampton Wanderers manager John Barnwell brought in their old player Dennis Willshaw as club psychologist, and if Manchester United had employed someone like that instead of a pretty basic character like Matt Busby, they might have got something more out of George Best. By the time they started sending him to a psychoanalyst it was too late, but again they can't be blamed since they come up as managers from the ranks of professional footballers and that's their life. The professional footballer leads a very limited life in an authoritarian world in which he isn't expected to show any initiative off the field and this is the kind of regime he is subjected to from an early age, so if he is not the most enterprising creature outside the game, can he be blamed?

Now we can perhaps turn to your novel writing. You have produced many titles since 1952, both novels and short stories. I know that William Walsh, Professor of English at Leeds and a strict Leavisite, in his book A Human Idiom *devoted a chapter to your work, praising it as 'cool and lucid, subtle and versatile,' that your work illustrates the Henry James conviction that what counts is what is illustrated. Do you agree?*

Oh, Henry James's marvellous cry, 'Dramatise! Dramatise!' as distinct from editorialising. I get utterly fed up with authors who tell you about their characters rather than showing you.

And your method of showing character – is it through dialogue and subtle uses of the idiom of dialects as well as of language generally?

I was reading this morning some incredibly bad short stories by John O'Hara in a book with a self- congratulatory preface saying, "It's years since I wrote any short stories and I'm still so goddam good." He isn't – the work is shallow and slick and knowing. He was a terrible blowhard, a disappointed man, but then we are all disappointed; I'm out of fashion at the moment and I've got a couple of plays going on at Chichester at the moment that I've always wanted to write but it's taken thirty years to get round to that. Scratch any writer and you find a paranoid: we're all horribly

67

neglected, desperately underrated, none of us have had our due and I'm as bad as anybody else but I try to keep up a public face which is somewhat less infantile.

What I'm trying to say in a clumsy way is that it exposes the poverty of dialogue written on its own. Henry Green used to say that he thought all novels should be written in dialogue because that's how he liked to write and he was a much more refined artist than John O'Hara though his early work was not to be despised, but I never liked his novels, very vulgar. Dialogue is of great importance but you cannot live on it alone.

And you would import into your narrative which was not dialogue a vitality which would charge the prose and keep your theme going between the stretches of speech?

I try to, and I use a lot of dialogue. I like writing stories in the first person which gives you the best of both worlds because if the story is in the first person then it is a form of dialogue. Perhaps I've become over-committed to that kind of writing. I'm pleased now to be writing plays but will continue to write short stories. The last novel I wrote, *Never Look Back*, about the rock world, is the only novel of mine, I think, to have been savaged. I thought more people would like it than actually did, although I knew it would be hated, but critics in this country are conceited and obtuse – there's my paranoia coming out again! The fact that the book was a reworking of the Orphic myth is something that eluded them all. When I published *The Olympian*, the only one of my novels which had great success in America and is still in print after twelve years, it was appreciated on every level by every person, from Mark Schorer to the American presenter of their *TV Today* programme who said acutely that it wasn't really about track events. It wasn't; again it was about the reworking of certain myths but no one in England saw it – even critics who praised the book didn't see that. They still thought it was a documentary novel.

The Olympian and The Comic and unhappy footballers past their prime all represent a contemporary type, don't they? The character in disarray and disillusion with little else under him once his career has ended. This is a way of describing contemporary man, is it?

Very much in *The Olympian* where I took the runner as a symbol of perfect futility, the complete embodiment of Faustian activity. What could be more insane in this mechanised age than to devote the whole of your life to an almost religious self-denial and even the abuse of one's body through steroids in order to run a short distance at a quarter of the speed of a pushbike?

Is it a substitute for something higher, a cult?

They think it is but I think it is a form of the restlessness of this age, an inability to be at peace with itself; man's alienation from his own body, his punishing of the body instead of enjoying it. I tried to say what I was doing, but if you do that over here they are insulted, and if you don't they don't see it.

You have also written Jewish novels and novels set in Italy. Would you like to say something about those?

I wrote two novels with a Jewish family background, *Diamonds* and *The Bankrupt* and with those I think I had said everything I wanted to in that way. The only other novel with a Jewish content was *The Financier*, which to me was a much more satisfying novel because it was trying to say larger things. *Diamond* and *The Bankrupt* still appear to be popular among library readers but I feel a long way from them now and they aren't the kind of novel I would ever want to write again but were the kind of novels I had to get out of the way so as to move on to other themes. *The Financier* was moderately well reviewed here but fell on its face in America. It can be read as the story of a gigantic swindle or, if you penetrate it, then it can be seen as another reworking of myth, each of the characters being a reincarnation of a Jewish clan of the 17th and 18th centuries, but that is a feature one doesn't want to include in the blurb, and accordingly nobody picks it up, but in this case they had more excuse for not seeing it!

And again was the dialogue in the Jewish idiom within the claustrophobic Jewish family and heavy paterfamilias?

Some of it, yes. One of the characters is the son of a rabbi and is a confidence trickster, has been to the London School of Economics and starts a movement called Creative Capitalism. Another character is an American called Jake Frank, the reincarnation of Jacob Frank who was a dubiously erotic figure in the 18th century and highly influential. Their forms of worship went on for two hundred years in Europe and is a bizarre form of Judaism in Europe. So the tale deals with that and at the same time is a parable of the modern world with Creative Capitalism's ethos being that Money is Love. If imitation is the sincerest form of flattery, then I was flattered by Richard Condon, the American novelist who took that as the title for one of his own novels later, without acknowledgement, the novel he called *Money Is Love.*

Your mention of the erotic prompts the question – what about sexuality in contemporary fiction? Is it something which would excite a novelist to try to understand it in contemporary terms? Is it important to you?

It is very important to me in certain stories I have written. I remember being attacked in the *Times Literary Supplement* for the 'coarse banality of the author's fantasies' in *The Financier,* but they were not *my* fantasies but those of the characters. There is a great deal of sexual activity in the book because the man Frank was an orgiast; and I have written short stories with erotic themes. There is some sexual activity in the two recent plays, particularly the one called *Old Masters,* but it is always a question of what one is dealing with. I would never import sexual scenes into a novel where they had no place. I remember J.B. Priestley writing about the popular novel which goes droning on in its middlebrow way and suddenly introducing a pocket of sex from time to time; that would not be the way I could work. In the new novel, *Never Look Back,* there is some homosexuality because I felt it belonged rightly to that story, but I found it hard to write about because I don't find it an agreeable subject to write about, but it was there and I introduced it within the context as sympathetically as possible.

Do you begin with a theme or just write and then something emerges?

Hard to know precisely. It's usually just being hit by an idea; in *The Olympian,* for example, I had a picture in my mind of a man and woman running; that was all. In *Never Look Back* I was intrigued by the strange phenomenon of the rock star, something that could not be explained in modern rational terms, in terms of Reductivism. And in *The Dying Of The Light* I was fascinated by the professional footballer who has fallen down on his luck and has suddenly become the people who have been living through him and, wilfully or not, exploiting him in his professional life, then totally discarding him, so that in a sense he is a man who has lived his life backwards; that is what interested me. The play, *The Old Masters,* is about the strange life of Bernard Berenson, and the possibility there of the old swindler being swindled.

I find it harder and harder to get ideas now, even for short stories, and one cannot tunnel them up. Journalism teaches you to be quick on your feet and working something up by free association or cross reference to get ideas, but I can't do that – the stories have to rise out of the depths.

But in your recent book of short stories, A Bad Lot, *the name story contained just about everything there is to be said about professional football in about eighteen pages.*

Oh, if it's that good I must promote it to a hard cover collection! It was written originally to be read on the radio programme *Jackanory.*

Reference is sometimes made to a 'metropolitan literary clique.' Is there one, and do you belong to it or despise it?

I think there is one; I think there is no doubt of it. I've been going now for about twenty-five years and in the early days I knew many people in London literary society and saw a good deal of them. Now I don't see much of them. There is of course a cliqueishness; for example, the other day in a Sunday paper X had written a novel which was given an extensive review and lo! X was a friend of the Literary Editor of that paper, and along with the review was an interview with X. I wondered what someone living in the provinces would make of that. But I realise that if promotion is needed then that's one way to do it and some writers have done it. English literary society is, I find, sterile, a matter of taking in one another's washing, and I don't find their company stimulating, the women in particular. Olivia Manning, a talented writer, lived in an aura of frustration, anger and resentment, sheer misery; it was impossible even to compliment her. She reminded me of the remark Saul Bellow made about the man who had so many irons in the fire he didn't know which one to brand himself with. Others are so conceited that when you meet them at parties you feel honour bound to sabotage them, send them up.

American literary society is much more stimulating, and there is more overlap with other arts, especially with painting, which doesn't happen here. Painters are much nicer people than writers, more physical and outgoing. No – I'm not so interested in meeting writers, because after all the best thing they do is to write, so that if I want to know about them I would pick up a story of theirs and I would get the best of them out of that.

Could I end by referring again to that question of the tension between journalism and creative writing, crucial in your case?

I think it is a key question. I always think of Ring Lardner, the American sports writer who therefore did not have to face the aesthetic snobbery typical of this country. He was admired for his journalism and for his short stories and his wild, Surrealist, one-act plays that Kenneth Tynan so admired, almost predating Ionesco. He was a fine example.

I have been greatly helped by sports journalism, firstly by making a good living by it and so being enabled to write novels in the way I wanted to, and secondly being able to transcend the narrow world of so many contemporary novelists – wasn't it Orwell who said in an essay that the typical modern novel was a novel about novelists? One has been able to escape that closed, middle-class world into a much more vigorous, unusual world even if in some respects narrow, and thirdly through journalism I have been sent all over the world, have been able to travel to countries I would never otherwise have seen, at other people's expense. I am obviously not the best person to pronounce on whether it has damaged my creative work but on the superficial level because of the intellectual snobbery of literary people, it probably has affected me. At a preconscious level they like writers to be surrounded by a mystique, as if they are 'different,' detached, so that if football is your subject, even if in a more individual way, then you are branded and will lack that deference shown to others. You will not become a sacred cow – I won't mention any names because you know the people I mean.

An interesting fact is that in the history of English letters since World War Two practically everyone has come through on a first book: William Golding, Iris Murdoch, Kingsley Amis, Angus Wilson, Margaret Drabble. Once that is achieved, the critics tend to be deferential, even those who consider themselves macho and tough, and much space will be devoted to reviewing the sacred cows even when the work is crap. As an American writer said, 'Don't read reviews – measure them.' If you haven't sacred cow status then you are up for grabs; if my last novel had been by a sacred cow, then critics would have taken the trouble to see what it was about. But there is no point in whining about this; you make your bed and lie on it. As the Latin poet Terence said, 'Habent sua fata libelli' – books have their own fate. Then dear old C.P. Snow remarked to John Morris who was then Head of the Third Programme that, "He didn't really mind what was said about his books because he knew they were being read in a hundred years time." I don't really know if mine are going to be read in a hundred days' time! All one can say is one hopes they will be.

Richard Hoggart (with Malcolm Bradbury)

(1966)

I am in the English Department at Birmingham University with Richard Hoggart and Malcolm Bradbury, both experienced lecturers in adult education in the recent past and now in the internal university world. As a raw beginner teaching adult classes at Nottingham as part of WEA and Extramural Department programmes in literature, an obvious basis for our conversation is the little book you produced, Professor Hoggart, called Teaching Literature. *You say at the beginning that an adult comes to such a class because he or she is dissatisfied with the terms of his or her life. Can I ask you what you found in all your years of teaching literature that such a course did for students of this kind? Do you think they were altered as people? As minds?*

Hoggart   In most cases there's no noticeable difference. I've heard people say, 'You can always tell so-and-so's students,' and I have known this to be a fact with a teacher who has a very marked personality, but whatever changes there might be are hard to see. Really good students do develop their capacity to talk about literature, to write better and discuss better, rather like what happens to an undergraduate. You don't expect marked change like that in most adults, but like good undergraduates one finds they do begin to learn how to express themselves more clearly. They also gain a sense of the *discussibility* of human problems, which is important, and the feeling that they are not alone, but just how that is mediated in their lives through their actions is difficult to decide. I believe it does work through, a kind of liberalisation goes on, but the terms of their life tend to remain as they were, so that this is a very long, slow process. What do you think, Malcolm?

Bradbury   It is difficult to measure what may be happening, but in almost every class there is a certain number of people who really do show a radical change, that is, their whole outlook is changed by learning to assimilate literature in terms that have been set up for them from outside. They are ready for this – this is the point – they are prepared and frequently they go on to a university; most classes have one or two people who finally become undergraduates.

Hoggart   I think that's true, though they are not the core of a typical class.

I'm glad to hear you say that because my view of an adult class so far doesn't include that type. I have two classes at the moment, one at Alfreton in Derbyshire which is full of bulky housewives who would go to a class on almost any night of the week no matter what subject was offered, and apparently enjoy their two hours there, but what it is they have actually enjoyed I'm not sure, and it is that which prompted my first question. Have they enjoyed the relaxation, listening to somebody talk? If so, then I'm at fault because I shouldn't be talking for so long, and I do talk too long. Which brings me to another question: you say, Professor Hoggart, that the secret lies in the method of question and answer. What is the secret of a good question? It has eluded me so far.

Hoggart   I can tell you that, if I was teaching all the time, I would just go like porridge. I think it is the hardest kind of teaching that prompts the question – to find the kind of question – that will give them a hand-hold to help them up; it's the Socratic method, obviously. I can't pontificate on that or tell you any secret; I know the general rules, that is, to find the point at which they are at and then hold out something so that they can make that leap for themselves. We've all done it at some time, but unless we are in constant trim we all have our own temptations to speak too long, to take over because we're in command of the subject. I have a friend who was much more disciplined than I am and seven out of ten times he could hit on the question. That's the trick – constantly to listen to yourself, deliberately.

But have you found that every member of the class suffers from the same defects, that they are trapped within their own world and somehow you have to get them out of a prison? Just when it seems that enlightenment dawns, the next week they're back in their preconceptions, so you wonder what you should have been doing between sessions?

Hoggart I've found that the most important thing is to fix on the text; if practical criticism fits in anywhere it fits in an adult class and it's a matter of tapping sympathies over a *succession* of books, that's the important thing. It's not enough to stop with one novel so that a group of people understand one novel; one needs to constantly broaden the field, broaden the experiences that are dealt with, to be consumed in an interesting cycle. You meet a class and send them away to read something else or more of the same book, and each class gains something at each stage. One likes to think of the week as a pause between the action, the time when the assimilation really does take place.

Have you found that the classes are usually good at relating whatever theme there might be in the novel under discussion with other topics and connections outside, in a way that young students never do? Is this helpful or is it an impediment to teaching?

Hoggart Oh, that is the biggest single advantage there is in adult classes! Other than the fact that you haven't got the unity of young people all within a disciplined system. But it has its dangers – you might end up having a chat about something irrelevant, so it is vital to be asking all the time of them: in what terms do they connect this with?

A word about the dullness of a lot of classes and the lack of expectations. We all know the kind of class you're talking about and you have to admit at the start that there are some classes with whom you will never be able to succeed. If there's a long tradition in a certain district where you are a part-time tutor or a brand-new fulltime tutor you might manage to convince them that you're a nice young man, so long as you don't concede too much, so that you're only a nice young man because you go their way. There are all sorts of classes; what emerges is a function of the character of the local WEA branch and the tutor – you make your own group over the years. Certain people will not come to your class but will go to someone they feel more comfortable with, and you will be scarred as I was – and I think Malcolm could testify to this. I remember one class on a housing estate who wouldn't move an inch, not an inch, and I was forced to give up that class before Christmas. I had another in a village which was full of country gentleman – the secretary always called me Captain Hoggart – and I couldn't do wrong; they were intelligent, middle-class but two of them marched out when I tape recorded them and they discovered that their voices had a certain Yorkshire timbre and this was a shock to them. The worst of all was a class in Hull which had been in existence for ten years and was a Communist cell! And because I wouldn't let them use each meeting as a discussion group about the Party, they reported me and said I wouldn't allow them to choose their own syllabus – H.G. Wells for instance – so that there was a confrontation and I had to stand aside like the bad lad, which ended with them saying let bygones be bygones – the Party had agreed to that. Next year we made a fresh start on new lines and got big classes after that. So what we're really talking about is that out of what looks like disseminated material there is a general sense of seriously addressing the work with good values, and on the whole with a good class, by Christmas there is some good work done.

But there is a sameness about so many classes: "Oh, Mr Gerard, not another one of those morbid novels." That word is their criterion, meaning – what? "I dislike it." Have you experienced that?

Hoggart   Oh, it's the standard English word, a word that's an OK word right up to the top of our society, right up to Parliament. We know people who have given evidence before the Pilkington Committee*, who were educated men and women of the world, BBC television people, convinced of the "morbidity of modern English literature." That word is one of the great folk words of English culture at all levels, hence if you had a class of MPs or of senior civil servants you would have this problem. It is an interesting insight into English culture, that word, because when they accuse something of being 'morbid' it means they have been deeply disturbed and that is good; they are disturbed by kitchen sink drama. What you have to realise

Committee on Broadcasting (1960)

is that whether in a WEA situation or in a television situation there are people, working class, middle class, or upper-class who prefer conventional art to art that sets them thinking, and when they see – whatever the adverts present – a threat of reality thrown on to a screen, whether a play of David Mercer or *1984*, the shock is profound. One has to say, yes, that is right, and then try to make it as effective as possible.

To see it as therapeutic?

Hoggart It's the shock of art at its best. Maybe they will say, "I like this because it is cheerful," and will taste it, and then you would get into a discussion about challenging art and conventional art. The word 'morbid' could lead into a very interesting analysis of the relationship of art to life and of attitudes in our society.

Having been pressured for nearly one term on this question of the 'morbid' – we have been reading Lord of the Flies, The Power and the Glory *and Kafka's* The Trial *– I was weak enough to announce a bonus for them. They were asking, "When do we get out of all this dismal stuff – what are we getting from it?" So I told them we would next read* Lucky Jim.

Bradbury Yes, there are different kinds of objections from different classes; I've certainly had morbidity as one such. I've also had the opposite, that the work has been 'too airy-fairy,' too detached from life, which is also another interesting word to deal with. I found it very hard to teach Henry James to one particular class which Richard knows, the class in Grimsby where there was a strong feeling that James's characters were irrelevant, didn't matter, because they lived in the world that was too 'nice,' or, in other words, unreal to the members of the class, and so one has to make the argument from that point of view as well, and this is the balance one is chasing all the time.

Would you say that the composition of classes has changed? Are there more of the formally educated type coming into classes now, as opposed to the cloth-capped image one had of WEA classes in their earliest days?

Bradbury   My feeling is that classes tend to be rather unfortunately elderly, and this is a disturbing feature of many classes, that people have been going to them for ten or even twenty years, which as Richard was saying creates the group – not, I think, in a good way; they don't let other people in very easily. There are other reasons, too, why youngsters aren't likely to join: a lot of potential adult students are educated elsewhere, but I think there is a change in the composition, in that adult classes tend to be used by teachers as a sort of refresher course.

Hoggart   True, and they sit there taking notes but on the whole are no better at making relevant intrusions into the discussion or critical comments than the others.

Finally, can I ask if you think the average adult student is prompted into doing more exploratory reading after a course?

Hoggart   I think most students probably do, though one can't tell, because the day after the course ends they may have left the area! But those I have kept in touch with – yes, they do more reading. I sometimes wonder if they have a sense of loss afterwards. If the class is going well and they think a lot of you and you have guided their reading extensively, then they often write afterwards asking for more suggestions, and this is because it has been for some time part of a continuous process occupying so much of their time. I do believe that if you have conducted a group for two years, that is, two years of a tutorial class, then that tells.

Did you take classes at the same centre for years?

Hoggart   Yes, apart from Hull. I used to try to break it up, but not if there was a big class as at Scarborough which was able to produce large classes and where I taught for seven or eight years.

The same students or did they vary?

Hoggart   They would vary; there would be some from a previous tutorial group, some would drop out on the way and we would end up with about a third of those from the first tutorial.

So there wasn't sufficient identity over the years to make it too cosy?

Hoggart   Oh no, you really have to resist that. There are stories of classes who have remained at one centre for eighteen years. I know two people in different parts of Yorkshire who have grown old at the same centre and some of their students who have grown old with them. That's something you need to discover, and you can make out a case defending it, but you can make out a lot of cases about its failures.

I would think you would grow pretty stagnant unless you were unusually resilient, in about three such sessions?

Hoggart   There is nothing more to offer, just as much as if you had the same tutor in your research three years as you had as an undergraduate at a university. There is always a change of tutor there, for one reason or another. But what happens is that they like the tutor, he is constantly marking their pieces of work and he enjoys working with them; it's all part of knowledge, as they constantly extend their information and knowledge. It's like a marriage, and ceases to be a Socratic situation.

Eugene Ionesco (1974)

Au début, cher M. Ionesco, je voudrais vous demander pourquoi le théâtre, pourquoi dès le début, avez vous choisi d'explorer la condition humaine, au moyen du théâtre?

Je crois que c'est le ... c'est un hasard ...

Par hasard!

Par hasard, ... c'est à dire que je ne veux pas faire autre chose que de la littérature, et alors, j'ai écrit des poèmes qui étaient assez mauvais, puis de la critique littéraire, et puis quelques nouvelles et puis une pièce de théâtre et petit à petit le théâtre a pris le dessus sur mes autres activités littéraires, mais j'essaye en ce moment d'écrire de nouveau des romans, parce que la création dramatique pour moi est ... écrire pour le théâtre maintenant, j'ai trop d'habitudes, il y a trop de clichés, des automatismes ete ... Alors je voudrais pour un certain temps me libérer de celà, écrire autre chose. J'ai écris un roman récemment qui a été publié, j'ai écris des journaux intimes; il faudrait un certain temps pour retrouver, pour réinventer le théâtre parce que tout ce qui est appris est mauvais; tout ce que l'on découvre est bon ou risque d'être bon.

Toutefois, je pense que c'est peut-être le théâtre qui est ma vocation littéraire la plus précise.Je me souviens qu'à l'âge de 12 ans, à Paris, on nous a demandé de faire une composition ... un sujet libre, et c'était meme avant 12 ans, je devais avoir 11 ans; alors, j'ai raconté ou plûtot, je n'ai pas raconté, j'ai fait dialoguer des personnages qui parlaient de je ne sais quoi, d' une fête foraine, la mère et le fils, etc. ... et c' était le dialogue, c'était une histoire dialoguée si je puis dire, j'avais donc inventé le dialogue. Alors, maintenant il faut que je retrouve cette fraicheur pour inventer le sonnet, pour inventer le roman parce que je considère que l'art, la littérature sont des remises en question de la culture, de nous meme; ce sont des remises en question et des explorations; ce qui est difficile en littérature, c'est qu'il faut aller de découvertes en découvertes, autrement on est perdu, autrement c'est le cliché.

On dit que vous êtes un des fondateurs du théâtre de l'absurde, pouvez vous le définir, qu'est-ce que c'est l'absurde?

Il faut le demander à Martin Esslin!

Qui a créé le théâtre de l'absurde?

Le théâtre de l'absurde vient de très loin. Je dis toujours qu'il vient de Shakespeare, puisque vous le savez mieux que moi, je cite de mémoire: Macbeth a dit "Le monde est un histoire racontée par un idiot, pleine de bruit et de fureur et sans signification … dénuée de sens et de signification." Voilà la definition du théâtre de l'absurde, elle est donnée par votre grand prédécesseur.

Croyez-vous que vous avez été le pionnier du drame surréaliste? Est-ce-que c'était un acte voulu?

Absolument pas!

Beaucoup de prédécesseurs?

Non, c'est André Breton qui est venu voir une pièce au Théâtre Récamier, une pièce que j'avais écrite qui s'appelle *Amédée, ou Comment s'en débarasser* et il m'a dit: "voilà enfin le théâtre surréaliste que nous n'avons pas réussi à avoir pendant … durant les années 25 a 30 …" j'avais beaucoup lu les surréalistes evidement; j'en ai peut-être été inspiré, je ne m'en rend pas tres bien compte. En tout cas, il a dit: "voilà 30 ans après le surréalisme, qui a donné tant de choses en peinture, en poésie, etc. … en littérature, voilà enfin aussi un théâtre surréaliste" c'est à dire que le théâtre etait en retard sur son epoque, de 30 ans en retard. Il y avait eu le surréalisme, il y avait eu la peinture cubiste et puis la peinture surréaliste, puis la peinture non figurative, il y a eu la nouvelle musique … dodécaphonique il parait … Il y avait eu le cinéma, mais, il y avait eu la psychanalyse mais le théâtre en était resté à la psychologie de Paul Bourget et à la téchnique du théâtre réaliste de la fin du 19ème siècle, on ne sait pas pourquoi.

Alors, on l'a fait, on lui a donné … nous avons réussi à lui donner un élan, ce qui a permis ensuite à d'autres de faire du bon théâtre et meme du théâtre plus intéressant et plus audacieux que celui que nous faisons. Seulement, je crois que nous sommes à l'origine de ce renouvellement du théâtre. Des auteurs comme Vitrac, les intellectuels et les écrivians se détachaient du théâtre. Ils considèraient que c'était une téchnique inférieure, probablement à cause de ce que l'on appelle le 'théâtre de boulevard,' qui était un théâtre facile, arrière, qui avait plus que 30 ans de retard, a mon avis plus de 50 ans de retard, parce que les pièces de boulevard ne faisaient que continuer les comédies de Labiche et les drames de Dumas fils; on n'avait pas progressé, ça n'avait pas évolué.

En ce qui concerne le théâtre, Brecht a dit "On viendra au théâtre trouver, comme un spectacle, un travail terrible et sans cesse par lequel il doit gagner sa vie et subir le choc d'un changement continuel." Ici, dans le théâtre, il peut se créer dans la manière la plus facile, qu'est ce que vous en pensez?

Je ne comprends pas très bien. Je voudrais connaître un peu le contexte. Quand est-ce que Brecht a écrit ceci? Dans sa periode de jeunesse ou plus tard?

Dans sa jeunesse, c'est ça.

C'est à dire c'était le bon Brecht, ce n'était pas encore le Brecht dogmatique; c'était le Brecht anarchiste ... oui, il était beacoup plus intéréssant à l'époque, mais c'est une phrase que je ne me comprends pas très bien, vous voyez?

C'est un peu compliqué, les idées.

Non, c'est difficile à expliquer simplement et puis je crois que l'expression est assez confusé. Je ne sais pas très bien ce qu'il veut dire.

C'est typiquement une expression marxiste dogmatique.

Non, non, ... au contraire.

Avez-vous vous même des opinions sur la question de l'art en société? Est-ce que l'art a un role indispensable dans la communauté? Ou est-ce que c'est une expérience en réalité rare et pour peu de monde, ... vraiment?

L'art est indispensable dans la société, justement pour prouver, pour illustrer le besoin que nous avons d'une activité libre gratuite et associale. C'est le but de l'art à mon avis, c'est le but du théâtre: montrer aux gens qu'ils peuvent se guérir un peu de leur angoisses et retrouver quelque chose qui n'est pas apparemement utile; c'est à dire, l'art est le preuve de l'utilité de l'inutile.

Et bien entendu, c'est une expérience rare et pour peu de monde, vous croyez? Parce que c'est une expérience un peu paradoxale?

Pas du tout. Tout le monde a besoin de cette liberté, autrement les gens seraient fous, aliénés, encore plus qu'ils ne le sont. L'art donne la liberté, donne l'humeur, donne un droit de controle aussi sur les choses, la libération, l'art est libérateur, il est surtout libérateur, c'est sa fonction; il exprime des angoisses évidemment, il exprime des ... il parle peut-être de temps à autre ... il parle même très souvent de problèmes familiaux, sociaux; mais ça, c'est le sol. C'est la terre d'où l'arbre monte et dépasse le sol, il dépasse la nécessité, il s'élève.

Alors pourqoi la classe ouvrière n'aime pas du tout le théâtre?

Si, mais on n'a jamais essayé d'aller dans les villages, dans les campagnes leur montrer du théâtre. Mais la preuve que les gens ne vont pas au théâtre, qu'ils ne savent pas très bien ce que c'est le théâtre, (la majorité des gens sentent le besoin absolu du jeu, de la détente, de la liberté), c'est qu'ils sont si nombreux en Espagne aux courses de taureaux, en Angleterre aux matches de football et de rugby n'est ce pas? ... on ne peut dire que le football, que le rugby expriment des problèmes sociaux, c'est au contraire un jeu. Alors les ouvriers les plus pauvres vont aux matches de football parce qu'ils ont besoin de cette liberté, et parce qu'ils ne connaissent pas le théâtre: il faut donc leur faire connaître un théâtre qui soit comme un jeu, parce qu'on les assomme avec le théâtre politique, le théâtre social, le théâtre Brechtien, le théâtre Marxiste; naturellement ils ne peuvent supporter ça les malheureux, ils vivent dans la nécéssité toutes la semaine et c'est la raison pour laquelle ce théâtre Brechtien, Marxiste, tendancieux etc. ... de propagande n'est connu et n'est aimé que par les intellectuels. Jean Vilar a fait une aiment et qu'ils continuent à aimer c'est le théâtre de boulevard; c'est à dire le théâtre bourgeois. Si bien que paradoxallement, c'est le théâtre bourgeois qui est le théâtre populaire par excellence; quand ils vont au théâtre de temps en temps, ils ne vont pas voir les pièces assommantes de Brecht, ils vont voir l'histoire de l'adultère ou une comédie etc. ... parce qu'ils ne savent pas qu'il peut y avoir un théâtre libre, d'ailleurs un théâtre libre ... depuis une dizaine d'années, un théâtre libre, un théâtre d'humeur, un théâtre de jeu, un théâtre tragique, un théâtre métaphysique, tout celà depuis une dizaine d'années, ça n'existe plus; il y a la propagande qui est bien embêtante. Dans les pays de l'est, on ne joue que très peu Brecht parce que personne n'y va. Il y a aussi des music-halls qui sont pour les ouvriers aussi une libération, sans doute.

Oui, mais vous avez dit qu'il faut intégrer le music–hall et intégrer le cirque.

Oui, il faut intégrer le cirque, et il faut faire du cirque. Mais enfin on commence à en faire. Alors on a donné une de mes pièces: *Quentin Rousseau*, puis une autre pièce devant des publics d'ouvriers qui se sont mis à rire à gorge déployée, des comédies, ils riaient sans connaître le théâtre tandis que les bourgeois gauchistes de Paris ont eu du mal à accepter celà parce que eux ne sont pas libres d'esprit, d'abord ils ont une culture, c'est à dire des habitudes de pensées, des habitudes sclérosées, et qu'il faut qu'ils s'arrachent d'abord à ces habitudes pour apprécier le jeu, qui n'est pas forcément un divertissement parce qu'il y a un jeu tragique; alors les ouvriers, eux, avraient beaucoup plus de fraicheur d'esprit.

Nous arrivons à la fin . . .Alors voulez vous continuer d'être dramaturge plûtot que romancier?

Je ne sais pas, ... on verra, ... je verrai, et vous verrez!

Enfin trois questions fondamentales, vu que vous êtes dramaturge, philosophe, pouvez vous ...

Je ne suis pas philosophe ou alors parce que tout le monde est philosophe, mais seulement dans cette mesure.

Pouvez-vous résumer en un mot: qui sommes nous, d'où venons nous, à où allons nous?

C'est le problème que je me pose depuis toujours et la seule réponse, c'est un point d'interrogation énorme, et en réalité, c'est le problème fondamental et c'est celà qui nous empêche d'être heureux malgré tout.

Et enfin, avez vous rencontré des Gallois auparavant? Que pensez vous des Gallois?

Je pense que le Pays de Galles, aussi bien que l'Irlande, aussi bien que l'Ecosse, aussi bien que le pays de Cornouaille, je pense que ces pays colonisés par les Anglais doivent retrouver une autonomie, non seulement administrative, mais une autonomie spirituelle et culturelle. Il y a beaucoup de cultures enfouies, détruites. Les Espagnols on détruit les civilisations de l'Amerique du Sud, les Russes ont détruit toutes les cultures juives du centre de la Russie, cette culture qui nous a donné les ascétiques, les pensées religieuses et philisophiques. La Chine a massacré les Tibétains et détruit la civilisation tibétaine qui était la seule civilisation métaphysique existante et je crois que toutes ces cultures massacrées doivent renaître, c'est absolument indispensable a retrouver l'élite et les sources rajeunies de la tradition et je crois que c'est le moment où l'Angleterre, qui ne donne plus rien , qui est en pleine décomposition sociale, économique, philosophique ... je crois que l'Angleterre ait besoin d'être colonisée à son tour par les pays celtiques.

Eugene Ionesco *(1974)*
Translation

Can I ask you first all – why did you choose the theatre? Why drama as a means of exploring the human condition?

Oh, I think it was just chance. I couldn't envisage any other form except the literary, and after attempting poetry, which proved to be rather poor, then some literary criticism and then fiction, I wrote a play; after that the theatre gradually overtook my other interests. At the moment I am trying to write another novel because my play writing is threatened by clichés, habits of thought and expression, a mechanical lapse into my customary manner, and so to avoid this I think it will be good for a while to write something else, to free myself! I recently published a novel *Le Solitaire* (1973) and a kind of diary, *Journal en Miettes, Fragments of a Journal* – I need some time to rediscover and reinvent drama because it's bad to return to what is already known and learned, while to go on making discoveries is good, or at least risks being good.

In spite of that I think perhaps the theatre is my peculiar vocation. I remember when I was 12 at school we were asked to write a composition on any subject, and I began a story or rather not a story but a dialogue between various people speaking – I forgot exactly what – about a travelling show. There was a mother and a son and their story was told through dialogue, a kind of *histoire dialogueé*, if I can call it that. I was making up dialogue. Right now I need to rediscover that same freshness by composing a sonnet or another novel because I feel that art, literature, is restorative, a form of cultural repair, and a healing for all of us, putting things in question and exploring; that's the hard task for literature – to go on from discovery to discovery, otherwise it is lost and becomes mere cliché.

You are described as one of the founders of the Theatre of the Absurd. Could you define the 'Absurd'?

You must ask Martin Esslin![1]

Who first created the Theatre of the Absurd?

[1]Martin Esslin wrote a critical work entitled *The Theatre of the Absurd* (1962) which conferred the name on this type of drama.

It dates back a long time. I always say it goes back to Shakespeare whom you will know better than I when I cite this from memory, Macbeth speaking of life as "a tale told by an idiot, full of sound and fury, signifying nothing." Life denuded of sense or meaning – that's your definition of the Absurd as offered by your great predecessor.

Were you the pioneer of Surrealist theatre? Was that something you willed?

Absolutely not!

Were there many progenitors?

Now then – André Breton[2] came to see a play of mine called *Amadeus, or How to Get Rid Of Yourself,* at the Récamier Theatre, and he said, "It's a Surrealist play at last, something we've not managed to have for the past 25 or 30 years." Obviously I had read Surrealist literature, and perhaps I'd been inspired a little by that without realising it. Anyhow, Breton went on to say that this was a Surrealist play 30 years after we had had Surrealism in painting, poetry and literature generally. He was saying that the drama was thirty years behindhand, during the period when we had Cubism and Surrealism in painting, then abstract painting, and in music the new twelve-tone system; there was novelty in the cinema, too, and new forms of psychiatry, but drama still remained stuck in the ethos of Paul Bourget[3] and the naturalistic plays of the late nineteenth century. Why, it's hard to say.

So, we gave it a new impetus which enabled others to write good plays, much more interesting, more audacious than ours. I would say simply that we were at the start of a renaissance in the theatre. Other playwrights followed in England, Germany, Italy and America taking our work much further, but we supplied the initial impulse, that's all; around 1950 there were a number of young writers in France including Samuel Beckett who was then about 40, Genet, about 40, myself nearly 40, and another very, very young writer, a member of the Académie Française, Paul Claudel[4] aged 70, but apart from Claudel and Vitrac,[5] most writers and intellectuals

[2] Breton (1896–1966) poet and critic, a founder of Surrealism.
[3] Paul Bourget (1852–1935) novelist of conservative tendencies who wrote naturalist fiction.
[4] Paul Claudel (1868–1955) dramatist.
[5] Roger Vitrac (1899–1952) Surrealist playwright and poet.

were not involved with the theatre. They thought it inferior, probably because of the tradition of the Théâtre de Boulevard, the commercial theatre, which was superficial entertainment and behind the times; Breton thought 30 years behind but I would say more like 50 because such plays were just repeating the kind of comedy that Labiche[6] wrote, or the tragedies of Dumas *fils*[7]. There was no progress, no evolution.

Brecht once wrote: "We come to the theatre to witness in a play a terrible spectacle in order to have life and suffer the shock of continuous change, and we have to make this happen in the simplest possible way." What do you think of that?

I don't really understand what he means. I would really need to know the context. When did Brecht write that, in his youth or later on?

When he was young.

In that case it was when Brecht was at his best, not the dogmatic Brecht; Brecht the anarchist, in fact, at a time when he was much more interesting. Still, as a statement it's not something I really understand.

A rather complicated idea?

No, it's a little hard to determine just what he was saying – its expression is confused. I don't know what he really meant to convey.

It sounds like a typical dogmatic Marxist idea.

Oh no, I'd say it was quite the contrary.

Have you yourself opinions about the place of art in society? Is art indispensable? Or is it a rarefied experience only for the few?

Art is indispensable, in order to prove and to illustrate the deep need we have of an activity that is truly free, unrestricted, not bound by social conventions. That is the real aim of all art, and especially of the drama as I see it, to show people that they can be cured of their anxieties and rediscover something which isn't apparently of any use, namely that art is proof of the usefulness of the useless.

Yet as an experience it is enjoyed by only a small minority.

[6] Eugène-Marin Labiche (1815–1888) comic playwright (*The Italian Straw Hat*), one of the most popular 19th century dramatists.
[7] Alexandre Dumas *fils* (1824–1895) dramatist and novelist.

Do you think so?

It is a paradox.

I don't think so. Everyone needs this form of liberation otherwise people would be even crazier, more alienated than they are now. Art offers them freedom, humour, a form of control over affairs. Art is liberation, a liberator; that is its function above all. It deals with anguish and tragedy of course, and with extreme situations, as well as with familiar problems, with social issues, but that is the very soil out of which the tree emerges and grows until it transcends necessity. It rises above all that.

In that case, why do the working-classes not like the theatre? At least not in England.

But they do. We have never tried to go into the villages and into the rural areas to show them theatre. But proof that people do go to the theatre and know very well what it is can be found in Spain where they go to bullfights, and in England where they throng to see football and rugby matches. People do have a need for play, for relaxation, just the need to feel free, and while football or rugby don't concern themselves with social problems they are recreations, and so the workers who have just as much need of that freedom as anyone else will visit football matches for that reason because they haven't experienced the theatre.

For that reason we have to bring them drama which is like a game because political plays bore them, especially that kind of 'socially-aware' theatre, Brechtian drama, Marxist plays – ironical, in a way. But the underprivileged won't support that kind of theatre because they live daily under the stress of necessity and for that reason Brecht's plays or tendentious Marxist drama remain unknown to them and admired only by intellectuals. Jean Vilar has done some interesting work in this field and has managed to attract a large public, but the playgoers who flock to the Théâtre National Populaire are Leftist intellectuals or the wealthy from the 16th arrondissement in Paris and the equivalent districts of London, Chelsea perhaps. But as to the popular theatre, as we call it, who does that cater for? Not difficult to see.

What the ordinary person likes, even those among the working class, the 'proletariat' who go to the theatre, is the commercial play, the Théâtre de Boulevard which is essentially a bourgeois theatre, the truly 'popular' theatre. Consequently when they visit the theatre from time to time they don't wish to see Brecht's tedious plays but rather something about an illicit affaire or a farce. They don't have any notion that a truly free theatre exists and has done for a dozen years or more, a theatre of sheer fun and games, and of tragedy and of metaphysics. It's the propaganda about it that is so tiresome. In the Eastern European countries Brecht is not put on very often because no one goes to see his plays.

And the musical hall has always been the theatre of the working-class, but you have said that musical hall and circus should be integrated into theatre.

Yes; circus and music hall should form part of it, and this is beginning to happen. One of my plays, *The Bald Primadonna* was staged before working-class audiences who received it with roars of laughter, heartily enjoying it as they did two or three others and yet without knowing it was 'serious theatre' while the Leftist bourgeois audiences in Paris took it amiss because they don't have the same free spirit. They have one notion of culture, certain habits of mind, a hardening of the arteries, and they will have to uproot those entrenched attitudes if they're to appreciate fun in the theatre which isn't merely an entertainment but is part of a tragic game. The working-class for their part have much greater freedom of spirit and can enjoy things unselfconsciously.

Will you continue to be a playwright rather than a novelist?

I don't know. We'll have to see!

Three final questions, fundamental ones. You are a playwright, a philosopher ...

I am not a philosopher except insofar as everyone is a philosopher – only in that respect.

Could you sum up for us briefly: who are we, where did we come from, and where are we going?

That's the problem I'm always posing, and the only answer is one enormous question mark. It's the fundamental problem and is certainly the one that prevents us being happy in spite of everything!

Had you previously met any Welshman before coming here to Aberystwyth? What do you think about the Welsh?

I think that the Welsh, the Irish, Scots and the Cornish people, the countries colonised by the English should recover their autonomy. I don't mean simply administrative control but their spiritual and cultural autonomy. Many cultures have been buried and destroyed: the Spaniards destroyed the civilisations of South America, the Russians destroyed Jewish culture at the heart of Russia, the very culture which gave us the ascetics and so much religious and philosophical thought. China has massacred Tibetans, destroyed their civilisation which was about the only metaphysical civilisation in existence. All these cultures ought to be reborn; it is absolutely indispensable to rediscover a new flowering therein, a rejuvenation of their deepest resources from their individual traditions. And I think it is time that England which no longer gives anything and is in process of social, economic and philosophical decay, I think it's time that England was colonised in her turn by the Celts.

G. Wilson Knight (1976)

I think it could be said that your great contribution to the study of literature might be summed up in the word 'interpretation' because you have been an outstanding literary critic – but also an actor. Your books like The Imperial Theme, Laureate Of Peace, The Wheel Of Fire, The Shakespearean Tempest, *have always had resonant titles which suggest the theatre. Is this how you would see your own life's work?*

I think I would. Acting and producing has always been nearest my heart. I didn't expect to write on Shakespeare at all at first; it was going to Oxford that stimulated me, but I had always been interested in Shakespeare and particularly in Shakespeare on the stage as a boy at Dulwich College, seeing Beerbohm Tree and Granville Barker's productions and living by them. They were my consuming interest as a boy, and as soon as the chance came I acted, at Cheltenham, and the British Empire Shakespeare Society produced plays for schools. My real chance came when I went to the University of Toronto in the 1930s where I hired a theatre, a little theatre, and put on my own shows.

Did acting come before your need to say something critically, to write analytically and look into the text?

I can't say it did because Oxford provided the initial stimulus before I had the chance to act in the big parts – but all that is just a question of time and chance, where the opportunity occurs.

Who were your teachers at Oxford?

My tutor all the time was Brett-Smith.

Did he implant the sense of mystery, because you have a deep sense of mystery? You have written about the lucidity on the surface and the problems underneath.

That was congenital in me; I don't think any teacher implanted it. One of the best impulses was when my brother Jackson Knight was with me at a performance of *The Tempest* and we heard Caliban's lines on music, 'Be not afear'd, the isle is full of noises/Come ye sweet airs that give delight and hurt not/Sometimes a thousand twangling instruments/Will hum about my ears, and sometimes voices … The clouds methought would open and show riches/Ready to drop upon me; that, when I wake'd/I cried to sleep again.' Hearing those lines spoken on the stage, my brother said, 'What does that mean?' It was one of those key remarks that awoke me to try and find out what it meant.

Who did you first explore in trying to find out what it all meant?

I think I wrote first on the *The Tempest* and *Cymbeline*. The last plays interested me but I wrote on the whole of Shakespeare a monograph which was chaotic, not good at all, in those early days soon after I left Oxford, and it was quite rightly not published. Then I got down to it again, concentrating on the last plays, *The Winter's Tale* and *Pericles* and *The Tempest,* plays I was deeply worried about, trying to find out what their inner meaning was, got that into a script then boiled it down into a little thing called *Myth and Miracle* which was published at my own expense – I wanted to get it established. The year after that came *The Wheel of Fire* on the sombre tragedies, which was a series of articles and papers, religious papers not literary ones; nearly all the religious denominations had their journals, and I had one article in each out of which came *The Wheel of Fire*.

What in sum was The Wheel of Fire *about? What sort of conclusion did you come to at the close of that book?*

That is a dangerous question to ask because my main business was writing on the individual plays and saying whatever I thought was just about them. Anything in the nature of tying up my results came second, and the danger is that it will be said, 'He is trying to prove this or that,' when I wasn't; I was simply wanting to tidy up the book. I had an article called 'The Shakespeare Metaphysic' which I don't think about now; it was a very provisional piece of writing about one aspect of it, but the separate articles on the separate plays are what I stand by still, interpretation of the plays, but I don't want it thought that the interpretations are offered in order for me to make an *argument;* that's the point. The interpretations stand on their feet.

I know the figures which have attracted you most have been Shakespeare, Byron, and Pope; not so much the novelists, and not Chaucer. Does this say something about you as a person, because to me novelists and Chaucer suggest the here and now, the prosaic, the everyday, the lack of that mystery you frequently refer to, the Otherness, the Supernature, which is perhaps less evident in say, George Eliot, than in the people who have attracted you. Would this be a fair comment?

Perfectly fair. I go to novels, if I go to them at all, for sheer entertainment – Neville Shute's novels for instance – but I go to the writers I have concentrated on for something more than that; they help me with struggles and torments and delights in life, but the average novel which seems to play on the surface of life I am not attracted by. For entertainment I find some of Masefield's tales appealing, easy books to read. The more difficult ones, George Eliot, yes, I read with pleasure as a boy – *Mill On The Floss, Silas Marner* – but I'm not addicted to them, nor to Jane Austen either, and I like Richardson better than Fielding for the simple reason that he is more dramatic.

In short, there's something about drama and the poetry.

Drama and poetry undoubtedly are my main interest, especially drama. I'd rather have drama without the poetry than poetry without the drama.

What is it that drama does to people? Why do they like to sit and watch people who never existed acting out a plot that never was in a time that simply was not?

I don't know, I don't know. I could give some reasons. I think basically I would go back to Nietzsche's *Birth of Tragedy,* which I regard as a great book, a tangled and untidy book but nevertheless the first half great on the nature of drama. I should say because I do believe in a hinterland to this life we live, an Otherness; I believe in its existence and it would be remarkably strange if it wasn't. If, according to Pope, his description of a chain of being from the animals to man where consciousness has reached its apogee and there was nothing beyond, it would be so extraordinary it would be hard to conceive it. We may be at the peak of the evolutionary process but our eyes are blinded to any amount of things that lie beyond. For this reason I like drama because according to Nietzsche they introduce us to that *Dionysian* Otherness and the Dionysian is the easiest way to explain it; it is some intimation of that through plays. It can take many forms but whatever form it takes it will surely have something in it that is wrong; you want it acted and then it can be shown to interpenetrate our lives at key moments, through dramatic action. That is why I think it *shows* us and introduces us to what is the truth of life.

You mean the actor while he is in the part and on the stage is in himself experiencing some kind of 'ecstasis,' a standing outside his ordinary self, a heightened form of the ordinary person going about his business?

Yes, entirely so. And I should say not only the actor but also a spiritualist medium is introduced to you as the onlooker at a play. They both put one hand out towards an audience while listening back to voices at the side giving them messages. That seems to me a common intention of drama, receiving messages and giving them out to an audience. The actor does this in his own way, getting a thrill from being somebody else. As an actor I am pretending to be somebody else, and it strengthens his personality, is an enrichment from unseen sources. We are introduced to the essence of life that way, I believe.

Recently I was doing *Timon* in rehearsal and was persuaded not to use a wig. I concluded after rehearsing a few times that this was wrong; I wanted to put on a wig because it helps change your personality, makes you feel you're making something rather than just being yourself. And that making something is very important, an enlargement of yourself.

And the audience, what of them meanwhile? Are they somehow partaking of this process?

I suppose they are. Their presence and appreciation lends the actor power, though one can't be sure of that, and that they should be there seems to be a necessity. There is a certain satisfaction from acting by oneself, but an audience is always implied; it needs to be seen and to be shared.

Do you see a poet then as something of an actor? I'm thinking of Pope – how does he strike you in all this?

Any poet is a kind of actor, doing the same job on a different level, for a different purpose and in a different medium. While writing, composing, he is doing just what the actor is doing, enlarging his personality, enabled to say things he wouldn't say otherwise, wouldn't perhaps understand at other times. Pope is a good example of that. He was an actor on many planes, keeping close contact with his public, and with rivalries and animosities, and all that he enjoyed, but when he was writing his poetry at his desk he became a different man. One can imagine saying to Pope, 'What gave you that thought?' and his reply, 'I don't know exactly. I hadn't thought of it before but I have to get a rhyme.' He is one poet who seems only able to think his thoughts in rhymed couplets; he couldn't think them in his ordinary self but in searching for a rhyme he *lived* the thought, and brilliant thought, which wouldn't be his own without the couplet. It happens with all good poets, too, in their different ways. It is extraordinary, almost defying comprehension, but it does happen. That is the way Pope gets his best effects, I think.

What about your own processes of composition – how do you set about it when you have a critical book in mind? Does it engage you for a long time before you sit to write or are you someone caught up in a wheel of fire, intent on getting it down?

It varies. I still find so much comes to me and I am persuaded of truth and validity – I rather wish it wouldn't, but new and exciting thoughts continually come, relevant to literature, and I have to put them down. If I am going to write a settled book, or even an essay or lecture, I first map out roughly, then write it out untidily, at random, then in some order, then correct it again and again in typescript and have pages retyped, and yet again in proof and have to pay for that! It goes through all that process. Whereas my brother, the Latin scholar and critic, although more sedate than I am, will write his stuff almost immediately fit for publication. I prefer to do a scatterbrained piece in appalling phraseology, then look at it and build on it and create from it, rather as Shakespeare created from his sources.

You have written the biography of your brother Jackson Knight, a classicist who specialised in Virgil. Has there been close rapport between the two of you?

It's difficult for me as one of the two to say exactly what happened. I put down a lot of opinions of other people about my brother, in the biography, and they made comments on our relationship which are probably more reliable than mine. For my part I would say he has been notable for making certain significant observations throughout my life which have helped me very much, sometimes solidifying what I may have been groping towards, as his remark during *The Tempest* initiated so much. Again I remember when I was talking of something in Shakespeare, he said, 'Oh yes, he treats his themes like solid blocks.' I had said that a play of Shakespeare's was often divided between two sorts of interests, and his reply made it more vivid. He had a great gift of inspiring people and helping them bring out their talents; he played his part by making remarks like that one, on my own work.

As for my side of it, my brother always said he was helped by the work I was doing. I suppose my theories of literature in a way affected him and possibly prevented him from taking certain lines he might have adopted if he saw that I had expressed them to be untenable. But I am not a classicist and so could only be of any help through my approach to the literature I was studying. I don't think I got much help from his written work, but through his conversation he helped me a lot

Another great critic contemporary with you is F.R. Leavis. How do you estimate his contribution?

I'm afraid I am not a good person to answer that because when one is in a sort of rivalry, one isn't a fair judge. I respect him greatly for having published a long defence of me against other writers who I felt had been indebted to my work without acknowledging it and who had written critically of it at the same time – I forget the details. All I remember is that Leavis published it because he thought it right to do so; I met him soon after and he said he had threatened to resign from the Board if they wouldn't let it go in. I've always remembered that. I met him earlier than that and we were friendly, but the way my work developed was not easy for him to accept. I couldn't accept his wholehearted denigration of people, but where he writes on someone he likes he is fine, but then most people are when writing about what they like. In writing about his dislikes he goes completely wrong very often: of Arnold's *Scholar Gypsy* he says he is enjoying an eternal weekend, scornfully, whereas he is 'envisioned on the heights' and battling against the snow, having anything but a comfortable weekend! For Leavis to say that – he is not facing the poem; he wants to make a denigratory remark and says the first thing that occurs to him. I don't like his denigratory side though much of what he says is no doubt justified, especially about modern poetry.

As I see it, he seems to be in a temper and I think he must be angry with himself because he hasn't faced the fact that there are many imponderables in literature which he doesn't admit, the spiritualities, the Dionysian qualities, whatever they may be called. They do not bulk large in the pages of *Scrutiny*. He is trying to interpret literature as a way to rejuvenate society without taking the one essential key, and perhaps he is irritated because he half knows this. That would be my diagnosis, fair or not.

We can't stray far from Shakespeare with you, so may I ask how you see response to Shakespeare going on in the future? Will his actual language become more difficult as we move farther and farther from the 16th century? Will

meanings grow more inscrutable or will audiences continue to be awed by his majesty?

I think there is a long way to go before we reach that stage. I can't think that a performance if well spoken could fail to appeal to an audience in a hundred years or even in five hundred years time. The main gist of the performance would be there, and the main gist of the speeches. On the other hand speaking as a student of Shakespeare, not as a linguistic scholar which I am definitely not, I do believe that we don't comprehend his language *enough*. However much we think we know it, we find ourselves again and again being caught by taking a word at its modern connotation, whereas in his time the word would have a different value: an example of that is when Hamlet says after his long soliloquy, 'From this time forth my thoughts be bloody or be nothing worse!' We all think he is about to be murderous, but although 'bloody' can mean murderous in Shakespeare it can also mean full-blooded, and so it means in Hamlet, not, 'I'm going to be bloodthirsty.' He wanted to outline a policy that is admirable, 'bloody' – virile, manly. Again in Macbeth, 'Bloody, bold and resolute,' all the three go together, a natural feeling of being manly.

Tucker's edition of the *Sonnets** first introduced me to the extraordinary trickiness of Shakespeare's words. Tucker's notes in his edition of the *Sonnets* are the best possible introduction though we have to be on guard when he goes wrong. So I believe that although the expert has to be careful even now, yet the basic truth and effectiveness are such that even in many years to come the speeches will be on the whole understandable. What I do deplore is the mauling he receives on the modern stage, the tricks played with his work, tricks that have nothing to do with the play and are of no help to anyone. I don't mind if a word is occasionally changed, to help the public, nor do I mind the cutting of Shakespeare, which is a practical matter – if the seats are uncomfortable then the audience might wish more to be cut! That is about the extent of my answer to the question.

**The Sonnets of Shakespeare; ed. from the Quarto of 1609* (1924)

David Lodge *(1980)*

David Lodge is Professor of Modern English Literature at Birmingham University, and under that aegis he is himself a writer; he writes fiction and he writes literary criticism so I think the conversation might be a discussion about both those interests. You have written Ginger, You're Barmy *about your life as a conscript in the army,* The Picturegoers, The British Museum Is Falling Down *and more recently* Changing Places. *In criticism you are interested in the way language works, particularly in fiction, and have written* The Language Of Fiction, The Modes Of Modern Writing, *and* The Novelist At The Crossroads, *a series of essays. You have written a book about Evelyn Waugh and have edited reprints of classics including Jane Austen's* Emma. *To deal with the fiction first: much of your fiction is a form of comic parody, so how was it that this appealed to you, that this was the way you wanted to express yourself?*

I think I discovered that vein in my first novel, *The Picturegoers*, which is about characters in a London suburb who patronise the same cinema, a Saturday night cultural ritual long since obsolete. It was a novel with a large number of characters and had elements of parody, for instance of certain types of film and of some of the characters, but I don't think either the comic or parodic elements were predominant in that novel, and were almost completely absent from the next novel, *Ginger, You're Barmy*. I would say that on the whole, the university novels are rather serious, earnest novels with religious or ethical themes, and what you have just described is more typical of my most successful novels, *The British Museum* and *Changing Places*, both of which certainly do use comedy and various kinds of stylistic parody.

Does this come from anyone in particular?

I suppose I owe something to my friendship with Malcolm Bradbury, and it probably lay there in me waiting to be tapped. We were colleagues at Birmingham in the early 1960s; he came there in 1961 when I had just finished *Ginger, You're Barmy* and he had been writing for *Punch* and had published one extremely successful novel, *Eating People Is Wrong*, a comic novel. We collaborated in writing a satirical revue performed at the Birmingham Repertory Theatre, in the style of *Beyond The Fringe*, and I got a lot of fun out of writing what were trivial revue sketches and the experience turned me to comedy. The next novel, *The British Museum Is Falling Down*, which has a religious theme, the problems Catholics face about contraception, a few years before I would have tried to treat seriously and no doubt disastrously, I decided to treat comically, and to provide another interest in the book, I brought into the story some of my own experience in being a postgraduate reader in the British Museum Library. The hero who is doing a thesis on modern novelists' prose style, finds that different novelists take over his sensibility as he studies them, hence different chapters reflect in parody the various writers he has been working on, so that there is a parody of Kafka, of Henry James, of Hemingway, and finally the wife comes into the novel for the first time with a pastiche of Molly Bloom's soliloquy in Joyce's *Ulysses*. I think that answers your question. My fourth novel was *Out Of The Shelter* and was a flop – I notice you didn't mention it which shows how little it was noticed! That was a straightforward novel, sober, with a single tone to it, and perhaps because that wasn't successful, I thought I would try the comic. Hence *Changing Places,* which has been the most successful of my fiction.

That deals with the American academic scene?

It's about an exchange between a British university teacher and an American, and grew out of my experience in going to Berkeley in California in 1969. It was a time when there was much student unrest all over the world, including at Birmingham where we had our own relatively mild and well-mannered sit-ins in 1968, and I went from this to Berkeley where troops were on the street and helicopters were spraying gas and martial law was in operation. There were similarities and also great contrasts between the two academic scenes, and I brooded as one does on a structure, a story that would incorporate a sense of this similar yet disparate cultural phenomenon, coming up with the idea of an academic exchange, something I had never been involved in. Once I had the basic idea of an academic exchange, the novel wrote itself and I quickly wrote the opening scene in which the two men on exchange pass each other in aeroplanes over the North Pole on the way to their destinations. Once the idea of oscillating scenes occurred to me, then the novel wrote itself. It was inevitable that they would exchange not only jobs but also wives ultimately, that both would begin to change and the American become more British and the Briton more American. To vary the predictability of the plot I decided to write each chapter in a different narrative style, one in the present tense, one in letter form and one in the form of quotations, and the last chapter is in the form of a film script, so that the stylistic parody which you mentioned comes into that novel, too.

There has been quite a species of university novel in the past ten or fifteen years, though the earliest was I suppose Lucky Jim in 1954. And novelists today often come from a university background: John Wain, Malcolm Bradbury, yourself – all university teachers …

And in America, too. Most important American novelists have taught or are teaching in universities …

Yes, there are the Creative Writing courses there, and their Writers In Residence. How does this affect your writing? Presumably you are Head of a Department with professorial responsibilities which must take up time from writing. Does this mean you have to be more disciplined about it or is it something you can use as material?

Firstly, thank God I'm not Head of Department, nor do I intend to be. I have a personal Chair which means I have no more administration than I had as a lecturer. There is a psychological problem as one gets older and more senior, with more responsibility. It becomes more difficult in the academic world to combine that with the intellectual freedom which a creative writer needs, the irresponsibility, if you like. I have tried to cope with this by being simply schizophrenic about it – I have my academic persona and my novelist's persona and I try to keep them apart. I don't teach creative writing in Birmingham although we have an optional course of which I approve and take an interest in but which I don't teach because I don't want to mix up the two activities, the two aspects of my life.

In other respects, if one has to have a job, and one does have to have a job because few writers can afford to live on their writing alone, then the academic profession if you don't find it inhibiting is a very convenient one since to a considerable extent you can control your own time, there are generous vacations in which to work at writing, and at the moment I have a lot of opportunity to travel on academic business, lecture tours abroad and conferences. All this is grist to the mill; provided the professional clothing doesn't become too suffocating, then it is a good position to be in. The writers you mentioned, Kingsley Amis and John Wain, probably did find it impossible to reconcile these two roles and so they decided to get out.

Does the fact that your ambience is a university affect your view of your audience or potential audience? Or is that not a question you want to be concerned with as you write?

It does affect it. I'm sceptical of writers who say they don't think of an audience; it is difficult to write without some idea of who you are trying to reach. It will establish the style, it will establish the range of allusions you can take for granted when you write. Primarily – and this may sound egotistical – I am interested in literary achievement, I don't have to write for money, I don't have to compromise, and without flattering myself that I'm a major writer, I like to think I have written a few books which will be worth the time of future students of English literature. Because I am a critic and a teacher, that will affect the way I write since I'm not writing to be a commercial success, but of course that is nice if that happens.

As a critic you have gone into the bricks and mortar of novel making in order to analyse the way in which novelists grapple with language to present their view of the world as literary people. Your Language Of Fiction *is not an easy book to read because you are putting over concepts which are not easy to understand. Did your interest in this peculiarly difficult aspect of literary criticism arise from your creative writing or was it something you began to be interested in as a student?*

I have been writing fiction as long as I have been doing serious studies of literature. The answer to your question is that my interest in the rigorous, systematic, formalist criticism does not arise out of my creative work but the two feed each other. Many find it odd that I'm such an analytical, formal sort of critic and a comic novelist at the same time; they seem to feel it more natural for a novelist to be an impressionistic critic, even polemical, than to be coldly analytical about the art which you then practice as a novelist. I think possibly I am precise in order to keep the two intellectual activities apart, but my interest in the strict linguistic analysis of fiction began as an interest in the thematic point of view, my postgraduate thesis being on The Catholic Novel. I gradually became more interested in a formalistic approach which came out in that thesis, and the criticism I do now is quite alien to most creative writers who find it rather sinister, repugnant, but to me because it is a very different intellectual activity I find it a relief from creation.

Perhaps we can talk about the circumstance of being a writer. Have you views about the employment of literary agents? Have you used one since you started?

Not always; I acquired one after my second novel. I think it's unusual for people to hire an agent at the beginning of a literary career, most often one manages to publish a novel or two oneself then realises that the financial and business side of it is complicated and that it would be an advantage to get someone to handle that, and so you look for an agent. Agents themselves are reluctant to take on unknown authors, so that it's the case that once a writer has achieved an initial momentum in a career then the agent will come in and help him run it. Some writers have a close personal relationship with agents, depend on them for all kinds of creative advice and consolation. I don't myself, and my agency is a big one with many different specialists which suits me because I have different writing interests. It is essentially a business relationship, and I think my own instinct for the literary possibilities of what I want to do is better than theirs, because after all they are concerned with hundreds of writers and I know my own work better.

Can an agent be of value to an established writer? You say your own relationship is strictly a business one, but what about a writer who is established in his career – can an agent be of real help later on or is it bound to be a routine relationship? One wonders why agents continue to be of use to established novelists.

To my mind the relationship between a writer and his editor at the publishers is a much more important one psychologically since writers are more interested in what their publishers think than what their agents think. What the agent does is to take on his shoulders the odium of negotiating financial terms for something which is a creative product. The novel has from its earliest beginnings been a peculiarly mixed form, a commercial proposition, a product of the market, and at the same time a form of literary art, and that paradoxical continuation runs right through the history of the English novel. What the agent does is to take from the writer the burden of thinking about financial and contractual terms and therefore his relationship with his publisher can be kept on the level of the creative. And the agent will be able to protect the writer against exploitation and normally gets him a better deal; he will know how hard he can bargain. For instance a good agent will secure a bigger advance from a publisher than a writer will do unaided, and it's not just a matter of getting the advance before the money loses its value through inflation but the more money a publisher pays in advance the more copies he has to sell in order to cover his advance, the more beef he will put into the promotion of your book. It isn't just a financial matter, it is also a promotional matter.

On publishers – would you like to say something about your relations with them? I think you have had more than one – was there a reason for that?

The main reason was that the publisher of my first and two succeeding novels disappeared, McGibbon and Kee. They were taken over by Granada but the actual imprint disappeared and the people involved set up another small firm. At about the time I finished my fourth novel, McGibbon and Kee disintegrated after turning down that book, partly because they were about to dissolve and my editor was about to leave, and that is always happening in publishing. Your editor, the person who decided to take your book and so has some faith in you, will be sacked or migrate to another publisher, and this is one of the hazards of an author's life. My agent then sent that fourth novel, *Out Of The Shelter,* to Macmillan, who published it, not a happy experience either for Macmillan or myself.

At that time Macmillan were experimenting with computer typesetting which they hoped would be cheap and quick, but at that early stage it was expensive and slow and inefficient; consequently, when the book finally did come out it was much later than had been planned, so that instead of coming out in the early summer of 1970 it came out in October, at the height of the season, and that is not a good idea without a huge amount of promotion because every publisher is bringing out their best fiction by their big names, and the competition is intense. So *Out Of The Shelter* had very few reviews, and was technically a bad production being badly printed by the new computer system. It sold about 2,000 copies and the rest were pulped and it has never been reprinted, so it is now a rare book! In consequence, when I wrote *Changing Places* and it was submitted to Macmillan they turned it down, giving as their reasons that because the first one had done so badly they had no hopes for this one. Two other publishers eventually turned it down before Secker took it in a longer form than it finally appeared after I had improved it by cutting it, and I have wondered since what Macmillan thought when that book became such a success.

What about reviewing – do you find that reviewers have the same effect on you every time? Do you receive the same volume of reviews each time?

It varies. Fiction reviewing is sudden death; either you are reviewed in the first two or three weeks after publication or you can forget it, whereas in America the reviewing process goes on for a long time. Also, in the USA there is the kind custom of sending the writer proofs of reviews before they are published, so that if it is a bad review at least you can prepare yourself, but in England you don't receive advance notices and so just have to wait and see.

I find reviews an agonising business because it is the only objective comeback you will ever have about the book, as distinct from one's family or friends who have personal motives for not giving you a totally objective verdict. One is in suspense. Again to refer to *Out Of The Shelter*, the reviews in the *Observer* and *Sunday Times* did not appear in the south of England because those papers were not distributed there that day for reasons I now forget, yet another reason why it didn't do well, and those reviews were short notices. From a writer's point of view it is important to be reviewed at all, preferably prominent reviews, and best of all to receive many reviews in a short time. That happened with *Changing Places*, a royal flush, as it was reviewed in every newspaper and weekly within about ten days, and it was the lead review in the *Sunday Times* and the *Observer* in the week before publication. There are sceptics who say that reviews count for five percent of the book buying, but from the standpoint of the author's ego and his sense of what his audience thinks of him, reviews are important.

Your next novel* is about to come out soon, so as an established novelist do you expect to receive more reviewing space?

To be honest, and whether critics like it or not, I would expect this novel to be widely reviewed because *Changing Places* was the first novel in which I could say, 'I made it,' and became a recognised British novelist. But if this new one is not a success then the one after that might well get not much reviewing space. Some writers, like some of those you have interviewed, Iris Murdoch for instance, are far beyond the point of ever being neglected; whether her books are liked or not, she will go on being widely reviewed and respectfully because she has built up a very considerable *oeuvre* with a considerable public. I don't rate myself at that level yet.

Fiction is now being written on a scale like never before, but can it continue in a world with so many other competing distractions and forms of communication? Fiction deals with the prosaic elements in life, and aren't these being taken care of in other forms daily?

I'm inclined to take the optimistic view. For instance, television hit the popular cinema much more than it hit fiction, and I think other media like television are to some extent parasitic upon the novel and films, to a large extent depend on novels for their raw material; half at least of Hollywood's productions come from screenplays based on short stories or novels, and

*How Far Can You Go? (1981)

many novelists and short story writers are conscripted for films and television. A story by John Fowles was recently dramatised by Malcolm Bradbury for television, and I thought it one of the most interesting bits of television I had seen for a while. Where the market has shrunk I think is in middlebrow fiction, once the staple of Boots lending libraries; writers used to be able to make a living out of decent but not very important novels, and that audience has been mopped up by television. Now there is the blockbuster at one end of the market – Harold Robbins, Stephen King, *Jaws*, that kind of thing, mass entertainment promoted on a large scale involving millions of pounds, and at the other end of the market, highly competent, serious literary fiction which is not making money for anyone and is impossible to live by, but a great deal of prestige attaches to that kind of fiction and it is possible for those writers to publish such fiction and pay their bills by other methods, like being a professor of English Literature.

People have been saying for so long that the novel is doomed because of cinema or television and still it goes on, and I believe more titles are being published than ever, many in tiny editions now, perhaps only 1500 copies, hoping that if noticed it might be taken up by a paperback publisher – almost cottage publishing. It keeps the form alive and I'm reasonably optimistic about it.

And the other side of that query: how much longer can the classics of the English novel undergo further scrutiny after a century and more of Lit. Crit.? Is there a point when they will be exhausted?

I think probably not. One of the criteria of a classic text is that it is inexhaustible. It is difficult to believe this and yet it is a common human experience that one never reads the same book twice, partly because although the text as an arrangement of words remains unchanged the context changes so that we don't read Jane Austen or George Eliot as their contemporaries did. We can't because we read them with a double perspective in which we try to recreate the context in which they were written and also bring our own context to bear on it, hence there is a constant shifting relationship between the reader and the text which literally guarantees that literary texts will go on yielding new meanings as long as people continue to read them. The twist to that is that criticism may never be final, which some academic critics are reluctant to admit.

Edward Lucie-Smith *(1966)*

You are a poet and critic, especially of the graphic arts. Can I ask you when you first started to publish your poetry?

The first poem I ever published was in the *Spectator* when I was sixteen or seventeen, apart from poems in the school magazine. I'd been writing poetry since I was 14.

And your first book of poems?

In 1961.[1]

So you are a poet of the late Fifties and Sixties, firmly?

I hope I'm not firmly anything; I'm the sort of writer who is perpetually in revolt against what was done last.

And what was done last before you, then, was the poetry of cool, clear statement, like Philip Larkin and the Movement poets?

Larkin and Thom Gunn were the gods of my undergraduate days, and certainly I began as a poet at the tail end of the Movement.

What are your feelings about Larkin?

I think Larkin is an extraordinarily fine poet as well as an extraordinarily nice man who has been turned into a kind of Pope of literature in a way he never intended and in a way I suspect he dislikes.

He is so self-effacing it must be painful for him to receive Queen's Gold Medals and such like trophies.

I don't think it's that painful. Larkin is a poet of a very English kind, the descendant of Hardy and of Edward Thomas and he has a clear idea of what he can do with his talent and he does it. But I don't think he is the kind of major poet who can give a tone to a whole epoch of literature. I think the worship of Larkin has been rather hysterical.

Would you agree that a major poet has to be a.) an innovator, and b.) prolific?

Yes, I would; I think that a very just description.

[1] *A Tropical Childhood*

So that, since Eliot, no one has emerged within striking distance?

I think I've had cause to think about English poetry and if I generalise, it will sound arrogant, but let me try. The Movement and Larkin arrived on a poetic scene which was in an exhausted condition; the only two poets writing in the late 1940s that were really interesting were Dylan Thomas and Betjeman, and Betjeman is a kind of archaist who stands at an angle to the rest of English poetry, and the Movement looked like a revolution but was really counter-revolution. Modernism had got itself into such a bad way that the Movement attempted to set up the old standards again, and in an England which was drawing in its horns, this was relevant and good. I now think that the Movement, and especially its alliance with the academy, is having a conflicting effect on English poetry and that there is a need for a major poet to give a lead, and that lacking such poets of our own, I think the most fruitful influence has tended to come from America, though, unfortunately, they have come in the form of sudden passionate fashions rather than as a process of slow absorption. The most important poets for the English writer seem to be people like Wallace Stevens and that very American poet, William Carlos Williams, and of course Robert Lowell. It is impossible of course to imitate them but to learn from them the breadth that American poets so often have.

Is America the home of great poetry at the moment? The names you mention…

The American tradition since the War has been much richer, more varied than ours, but it's impossible for a poet to write as he pleases without being exiled from the literary community. In England there have been only two generations of poets: the Movement and then, with Tom Gunn linking them, there has been the post-Movement, recruiting Ted Hughes, George MacBeth and Peter Porter, which is a rougher, hurley-burly poetry. But this is not a very wide range; a poet like MacBeth has tried hard to extend quite consciously the range of English poetry, and I wish more poets would do that.

Why does American poetry seem so much more towering than ours, more universal? Is it because they were late on the scene?

I think it is simply a matter of creative energy. If you consider the situation of the leading English poets, you find that they are based on a very small *oeuvre* and a small stylistic range. Larkin has published to date just two books, Ted Hughes two books and a children's book, MacBeth two books and a few pamphlets, Porter just two books. There's no figure comparable with the Americans: look at Stevens' collected volume, a great fat book, product of a whole lifetime. There is nobody living in England like that, and even the senior British poet now that Auden is resident in America – that is Robert Graves – has an extraordinary thin quality, a difficult poet but one of limited scope.

You were at Oxford so that you didn't come under the influence of the Leavis school.

I came out of Oxford into The Group, more or less, and The Group, even though I ran it for such a long time, is basically a Cambridge institution, founded by Philip Hobsbawm, one of Dr Leavis's pupils, and the whole way of thinking was very much governed by Cambridge criticism, the method of discussion, and that criticism was directed not at the works of the past but of the immediate present, and therefore I wouldn't claim that I have escaped from Leavis's clutches at all. I don't agree with much of what he says but the influence was salutary. I gave up running The Group because firstly I didn't have the time, but secondly I thought that our discussions had reached an impasse and that we were repeating ourselves.

Tell me more about The Group – was it a club meeting regularly?

I have to be careful about defining The Group because it has got itself a bad name. The Group started off as a number of unestablished poets who used to meet at Philip Hobsbawm's house once a week, and at each of these meetings one poet would read his own poems which were discussed freely by all present. What happened was — and the way The Group was kept together was by mailing list — the poets due to read duplicated their poems beforehand so that they could be seen in advance, and anyone receiving a copy was entitled to come, and if they rang the Chairman in time before a meeting, they could bring their friends. While The Group's mailing list even in its most expansive days was not more than a hundred, I suppose there must have been three or four hundred people who had attended Group meetings, so it's difficult to define as an institution because it was really a flow of people through a particular process.

And was it poetry reading and discussion followed by a re-examination of the aesthetic criteria of the time, presumably Scrutiny *criteria?*

I wish it had been that. In fact the scope was narrower – what happened was that people were made aware of two things which were of help to unestablished writers, one that made it clear to them how much of their work was private, how much people could misread and wouldn't understand, and this in turn meant that anyone who embarked on a poem of deliberate obscurity knew what they were doing and it tended to cut away careless writing. The other thing was that it was made plain that a poem was something which could and ought to be examined in the clear light of day, that it wasn't a magic and mystery, too delicate to be touched, but a work of art which could be roughly treated and still survive. I think the great flaw – and here I may be betraying my old friends – the Leavisite method led to an insistence on naturalism which in the end led to an unhealthy condition, that everything had to fall into the convention of the poem as a *genre* picture.

The Critical Quarterly *carried two articles on poetry which stand out in my mind, one by yourself, 'The Tortured Yearned As Well' and the reply to it by Richard Kell, 'The Poem Itself.' I don't know if you can recall them but Kell seemed to think you regarded poetry as a social activity and he was trying to maintain that the poem acted in a different way, that it was a slow-acting agency which only in the fullness of time made any change to a person, almost like meditation; that poetry in the social sense could be replaced by a sermon or a leader article. How do you feel about that?*

My comment would now be that in a sense we agreed with each other and didn't know it. That article was written at a period when my views were rather different; I was much more enamoured of the naturalist convention than I am now, and the article was written in a slightly confused state of mind. I still think, however, that it is nonsense to maintain that any form of artistic activity doesn't have social connections; it is an important aspect of works of art that they are symptoms of society, that they reflect society willy-nilly, and I would also now say this, a more difficult idea, that the social function of art differs from age to age, that art doesn't always fulfil the same function or conform to the same standards, that its place in society shifts about in the most disconcerting way, that it may do one thing in one society but quite another in a different society.

When you left Oxford what did you do next?

I first did my National Service as an Education Officer in the RAF, and then entered an advertising agency where I still work. I've been in advertising ten years.

What about advertising then? Have you views on this or are you neutral about it after ten years in it?

It's interesting that people still distrust advertising but that distrust has become less vocal and sure of itself; the moral imperative that used to be applied by literary people to advertising has become less imperative. Advertising has had two practical functions as far as I am concerned, apart from earning my living. One is that it did teach me a lot about how to write, and while people criticise advertisers' prose, it taught me directness and not to mess about but to get on with writing rather than to indulge in creative pangs. The other point is that as an art critic it has been an advantage to work in advertising over the past ten years when the relationship between advertising and the visual arts has become so crucial, so that for example I was uniquely well placed to understand pop art.

Advertising as a visual art, but advertising as a literary art seem to be worlds apart, do they not?

They used to be, but this conference I've been attending makes me wonder because many of the techniques used in poetry are advertising techniques: the way that words are set out on the page, use of typography, were invented by avant-garde artists and fell into the hands of the advertisers who have always used graphic devices in order to get the words across quickly with the right rhythms.

Certainly on the visual side – how many people would have bought a Dufy, but if you plant it on a pair of briefs then Dufy will be worn.

Well, I think that pop culture which is basically industrialised fashion – that is, fashion in the machine age, democratic, immediately available and cheap, instant fashion – in fact, is another aspect of pop culture. With its insatiable demand for ideas, advertising has borrowed from the arts with increasing avidity, and pop art was no sooner in the galleries than it was in the shop window.

Do the motives behind advertising disturb you?

I think they must disturb anyone, except that selling things has been a human activity for a very long time, and if pop culture is industrialised fashion, advertising is mechanised selling, devices which make things more widespread, instantly available; instead of a flock of salesmen, there is an advertisement. The one comment I want to make which I do find upsets people is that people who are unwilling to accept the economic power of advertising are very silly, because advertising is one of the props of our industrialised society and enables the volume of production to be kept up, which means cheaper merchandise, but it is often better that people should buy slightly more than they need because this keeps the cost down to the point where it is cheaper for them than if people bought just *what* they needed – do you see what I mean? I think that those who have an uneasy conscience about advertising suffer from a deeper-rooted malaise about the society in which they live and about the part which they play in it, but attack the symptoms while unwilling to go to the cause. They are willing to accept the benefits of a managerial capitalist society based on a highly industrialised economy and unwilling to face the consequences of their case.

How does an advertising office work? Are you allowed complete scope for your own creative ability in preparing copy?

In theory one is, but in practice, writing copy is like being a junior monk in a Byzantine theological college. I've always been able to understand how they fashioned the theological debates in the Byzantine Middle Ages after having attended an advertisers' conference where people go over and over the most trivial points as if they were quoting the Creed, whereas the casual reader will never notice whether the word 'une' or 'two' was used at a particular point.

Are there many creative writers in the advertising machine?

My own agency for some reason has a lot of poets in it, three at the moment, and it has employed two others that I can think of. I can only think of a small handful of creative writers who work in advertising agencies, far fewer than there were before the war.

To what extent does your mind-work during a working day differ from the mind in your own study at home after the day's work?

That assumes that I separate the activities, when in fact I don't. I scribble on odd pieces of paper all day long. I write something in the office and switch back and forth from one kind of writing to the other, and lead too busy a life to confine myself to a study where I am 'a poet,' and anyway that is against my present feeling that literature has a kind of gaiety and impulse and even frivolity which ought to be preserved at all costs; if it isn't fun to do it isn't worth doing.

So that we might have an Edward Lucie-Smith stanza in a Nescafe advert?

That wasn't quite what I meant, but I'm quite capable of keeping a notebook on my desk and scribbling down ideas on a busy day in five minute breaks from doing other things.

Was it difficult for you to shrug off the work of people like Denys Thompson and F.R. Leavis when you entered the advertising world? I'm sorry to nag at this, but so powerful was their blast against the whole advertising ethos – one of their criteria, wasn't it?[2] – that your attitude surprises me.

I'm not familiar with that side of Leavis, rather with his literary criticism, otherwise I've avoided it because I work in advertising, but it does seem to me from what I know that like so many prophets of doom they will not offer positive solutions or tell you what will replace the managerial capitalist society supported by advertising which I've been describing, nor will they tell you how their notions can be economically run when the millennium comes. If I might enlarge on this: they have a vision which goes back to your local hero, D.H. Lawrence, a vision of life in the country, a kind of anarchism, rooted in the soil, in doing things for oneself with one's own hands. But to bring this into an England with its present population, you would need to start by machine gunning three quarters of the population. In order to support itself at its present population levels and those which are likely to come, our society must be a society of machines; it's impossible to think otherwise, and this means that the kind of good life which Leavis and Thompson put forward is a dangerous fiction, that what we have to do is to accustom people to live in the new style of life which their very multitude imposes and which our democratic criteria impose, that is, everyone is entitled to a decent level of living and where after all nobody starves. So, to look to the past of the hand-made – maybe I'm unjust in saying that – seems to be foolish.

I can even envisage a future and find it bearable where the hand-made work of art, the last symptom of the craftsman, is also abolished. The question I ask myself is: suppose one were asked to destroy a marvellous

[2] *The Voice Of Civilisation* (1943)

Rembrandt, one would refuse even if the reason was that it should be destroyed because not everybody could enjoy it, an extreme form of egalitarianism which we sometimes hear in political terms. But if the choice was to keep the Rembrandt and have the people deprived of the aesthetic sensation, then I would destroy the Rembrandt because what is important to preserve is the capacity to feel aesthetically and the instruments of this may have to adapt themselves to a new condition of society. One must envisage this. And one of the most interesting things about works of art, as in the Concrete Poetry exhibition we have just seen, is that they are the originality of life, not in the materials and how they are used but in the *ideas,* and I think this is the way that art is to go, and that is to cut across Denys Thompson's approach as I understand it. This is also the reason that I think it misbegotten to try and formulate means of discrimination amongst popular artefacts like pop songs, since the criterion of pop music is that it's new, that it appeals for the moment and is a temporary work of art and operates in a different fashion from a real work of art.

Would you like to attempt a prophecy on the future of poetry in the 1960s? How do you think it might go after the Movement has died away?

I think at the moment there is a widening split between the official view of the literary world, the official view of what poetry is, and the poetry that is being written. The attitude of established writers is to say that Concrete Poetry is not poetry at all or that the Beat poetry being written in provincial towns is not poetry either, so that there is an unofficial literary world as seen at this conference, and the official literary world, and not many people bridge the two. I think that all the writing since 1945 is going to be put through a severe test of relevance. I detect among young people an impatience with English poetry and indifference to its products which to me as a writer is chastening and frightening, and I think we are on the verge of a shake-up. What will happen next I don't know but the literary situation is more unstable than it has been for many years.

Hugh Macdiarmid *(1966)*

The Watergaw

Ae weet forenicht i' the yow-trummle
I saw yon antrin thing,
A watergaw wi'its chitterin' licht
Ayont the on-ding;
An' I thought o' the last wild look ye gied
Afore ye deed!

There was nae reek i' the laverock's hoose
That nicht – an' nane i' mine;
But I hae thocht o' that foolish licht
Ever sin' syne;
An' I think that mebbe at last I ken
What your look meant then.

Crowdieknow

Oh to be at Crowdieknow
When the last trump blaws,
An' see the deid come lowpin' owre
The auld grey wa's,

Muckle men wi' tousled beards
I grat at as a bairn
'll scramble frae the croodit clay
Wi' feck o' swearin'

An' glower at God an' a' his gang
O' angels i' the lift
– Thae trashy bleezin' French-like folk
Wha gar'd them shift!

Fain the weemun-folk'll seek
To mak' them haud their row
– Fegs , God's no blate gin he stirs up
The men o'Crowdieknow!

That was Hugh MacDiarmid reading two of his poems. MacDiarmid is thought by some to be Scotland's greatest poet since Burns and like Burns he writes in Lallans, the Lowland Scots dialect. I'm with him on a grey Sunday afternoon, setting up the tape recorder in a small, unpretentious, single bedroom of a hotel. He is sitting on the bed, and I hope he is going to start talking to me about Scottish poetry and about this peculiar language which he has made very much his own, having revived it after it fell into disuse. It isn't Gaelic. Would you like to say something about it?

Some very great poets wrote in Lallans, or Scots, in the 15th and 16th centuries, but after that, and more particularly after the Union of England and Scotland, it degenerated into dialect. English established a virtual monopoly. Even today in our schools and universities, English is taught, English is the language used, English Literature is taught; Scottish Literature is not taught. Robert Louis Stevenson said there were no two adjacent countries so utterly different than Scotland and England, and that is true. After the Union, the great majority of Scottish writers acquiesced in assimilation to English standards and adopted a defeatist attitude to writing in Lallans. I never contemplated writing in Scots until I was demobilised from the Army in 1920 when it occurred to me that we had been fighting a war ostensibly for all nations, but that I knew nothing about my own country, Scotland, so I applied myself to a study of Scottish literature and the Scottish language, Gaelic and Scots, and acquired the kind of knowledge of a language which one acquires in studying for a degree of a university. Suddenly, quite unexpectedly, I found I could write better poetry in Lallans than I could in English. I can't explain it at all. It seems that the words themselves as I got to know them were capable of tapping deeper sources in my own nature than any English words could reach. However that may be, it is the case that I found I could write very much better poetry in Scots than I could ever hope to write in English.

What about the two poems you read? Could you explain them?

I'm pleased to do that – most of the words would be unknown to the average reader. A water-gaw is not a rainbow but the broken shaft of a rainbow sometimes seen among storm clouds. T.S. Eliot said that Scots was the only language in Western Europe that could not be translated into English. Any translation of poetry into another language entails considerable sacrifice, but any attempt to translate Scots poetry into

English entails much greater sacrifice, I think. Now what the poem says about the broken shaft of a rainbow is that one wet, early evening in the sheep shearing season in July when the shorn sheep are trembling with cold, I saw the broken shaft with its trembling light beyond the downpour of the rain, and I thought of the last wild look you gave before you died. The next two lines are difficult to translate at all: there was no smoke from the skylark's nest that night, which means it was a wild and stormy night and my heart was wild and stormy too, but I have thought of that poorish light ever since then and I think that at last I know what your look meant then.

Crowdy Know is the name of a graveyard in Dumfriesshire, the shire where I was born, and a lot of my forebears are buried there. What the poem says is, 'Oh to be at Crowdy Know when the last trumpet blows, and see the dead come leaping over the grey walls. Big men with beards I wept as a child, scramble from the crowded clay' – there's a lot of swearing – at God and all his gang of angels in the sky those crashing, blazing, trench-like people who'd made them move. And then the womenfolk will try to make them keep quiet; 'struth, God's not afraid if he stirs up the men of Crowdy Know.' It's difficult to get an exact equivalent – I couldn't translate it for the moment.

What about Scots Gaelic itself? Isn't that an even more ancient Scottish tongue and didn't you ever think of writing in that language?

I hadn't it natively. I was born in the Border country of Scotland and so wasn't a native Gaelic speaker. I've translated a lot from it, but it's a big difference as far as poetry is concerned if it's your native language, the one you learn at your mother's knee, and I didn't get it that way. But I know Scots Gaelic. It's a curious thing that the Gaelic-speaking population of Scotland, those who only have Gaelic, a few thousand, have begun a Renaissance of Gaelic poetry in the last few years. We have had three or at least two of the finest Gaelic poets ever, certainly since about 1745 and the Rebellion, when we had a flowering of Gaelic poetry with men like Alastair McAlister and Duncan Macintyre, two of the greatest Gaelic poets of all time. Today there is Sorley Maclean and George Campbell Hayes and Derek Thompson, all poets of the highest calibre. How to explain the sudden emergence of poets of that rank out of a language virtually at its last gasp, is a difficult matter. I believe it's possible we may have a general Renaissance of Scots Gaelic.

And what about your own medium? Someone coming upon your work from the outside world would immediately think of Burns – was he an influence on you as you began to write? He was the born progressive, the rebel, and you are of course a Communist who thinks in these terms, of the hope of a better world. Are these the result of studying Burns, or is he an unconscious influence?

We got nothing at school or elsewhere about Scottish literature until I was demobilised in 1920. I knew only the odd song or two by Burns and a few of the Border ballads, but I'd no idea of the separate Scottish literary tradition. Only after I applied myself to it, did I understand it. I'm not sympathetic to Burns, a song-writer, a refashioner of old songs, but not in my opinion a great poet, and far from being the greatest Scots poet. The greatest Scots poets were William Dunbar, Robert Henryson, and by studying their work I set myself two problems: I wanted to recover the independent Scots literary tradition at its highest point, and I also wanted to use Scots for high poesy, not for sentimental dogs or facetious verse or doggerel. After all, in the 15th century, Scottish poetry had a technical complexity, an ability to address itself to all kinds of subjects, that English poetry didn't acquire until Swinburne, perhaps. Some of the poems of Dunbar in their intricacy and their rhyme schemes are only comparable to the best Welsh poetry; there was no equivalent in English poetry until you come to Swinburne. So, there's always been a prejudice in English literature against what is called 'dialect' writing, and much writing in English in dialect, the Lakeland dialect or Yorkshire dialect, is at a pretty low level. It may have a parochial interest and there may be reasons why people want to perpetuate it, but it doesn't attempt any great poetical task, and I contend that Scots is not a dialect but a language, and no matter how low it has fallen, I have wished to restore it to its pristine place. So we started what is called the Scottish Renaissance movement …

Who is with you in that?

Quite a large number: Neil Gunn, the novelist; Edwin Muir, the poet, to start with though he repudiated it later on; Lilian Jefferies; John Ferguson; Marion Anders; Helen Cruickshank and many others. When we started that, the idea was to stimulate literary development, literally in Scots, but also in Scots Gaelic and in English, and as a matter of fact, though I'm best known as a writer in Scots, I've written poems in English and for the last thirty years I have scarcely written in Scots at all. I did what I could in

Scots in lyrics, but there was a displacement of my intellectual interest about thirty years ago, and I found it impossible to keep on writing lyrics – it became a trick which I didn't want to fall into – and instead I began writing extremely long poems in a multi-linguistic medium, with an English basis but introducing elements of all kinds of languages. That was necessary as far as I was concerned because of a breadth of interest in many subjects, the sciences and so on, and I didn't find Scots sufficiently malleable, but I believed that that multi-linguistic diction was a necessary detour for me, but that I would come back again to Scots to devise a kind of Scots that could be used in the kind of themes which occupy my attention now.

I'll ask you to read one of your poems in English now, though I must say that on the printed page it looks more insipid and anaemic than Lallans. Please carry on.

This is a poem called 'Island Funeral,' a funeral on a Hebridean island in the west of Scotland. I'll read just the first verses:

> The procession winds like a little snake
> Between the walls of irregular grey stones
> Piled carelessly on one another.
> Sometimes, along this winding track
> The leaders are doubled back
> Quite near to us;
> It is a grey world, sea and sky
> Are colourless as the grey stones,
> And the small fields are hidden by walls
> That fence them on every side.
>
> Seen in perspective, the walls
> Overlap each other
> As far as the skyline on the hill,
> Hiding every blade of grass between them
> So that all the island disappears
> One jumble of grey boulders.
> The last grey wall outlined on the sky
> Has the tracered effect
> Of a hedge of thorns in winter ...

Perhaps you would say something about the literary people you have met in your life?

I've been fortunate in meeting some of the finest poets contemporary with myself. I knew most of the writers of the Irish Literary Revival, in particular Yeats, the greatest poet writing English in my lifetime. I knew Dylan Thomas, and R.S. Thomas, and Kate Roberts. T.S. Eliot I was friendly with over a long period of years, and in the 1920s I was interested in Major Douglas and his Social Credit movement and the paper that promulgated his ideas, the *New Age* edited by Orage, which I think the most brilliant paper published in my lifetime; I knew Orage well and acted as literary editor for that periodical for a long time, and through it I met various people who were interested for whatever reasons in Douglas's Social Credit, among whom were Eliot and Ezra Pound.

What did you think of Ezra Pound?

When he celebrated his eightieth birthday I had the privilege of contributing to a *Festschrift*, and I said then and have no hesitation in saying again that I think he is the greatest poet in the modern world. I know his work is difficult, but as a literary critic and an absorber of various traditions of poetry into himself and giving them out again in an enhanced form, he has had no equal. I know he broadcast on behalf of the Italian Fascists and that he got into trouble with the authorities in his own country as a consequence and was held for some time in a lunatic asylum, but I don't doubt for a moment that he was the only sane man in the United States at that time. Ha! Ha!

What about the Welsh poets you mentioned, particularly Dylan Thomas – did you find you had fellow feeling?

I liked him immensely as a man, and Caitlin, his wife whom I knew prior to Dylan knowing her, through Augustus John the painter whom I knew well. I wasn't sympathetic to Dylan's poetry. He drew too largely on Old Testament sources and his ideas about sex among other things were antipathetic to my own ideas, but he was a young man and I felt he had enormous potentiality. His early death was tragic but he was misrepresented as an alcoholic – he wasn't what any Scotsman would call an alcoholic! He hadn't the physique for it, to start with, and he didn't drink spirits, only beer, and was no great consumer of that. When he went to America the overwhelming hospitality shown him included drinks with which he was unfamiliar and which had a bad effect on him resulting in his death. He himself was *not,* definitely not, an extremely heavy drinker.

Alright then – who was the greatest man you have met?

The greatest man I have met is Saunders Lewis, the Welsh Nationalist leader. He had a profound effect on me over the years. A wonderful speaker. In Scotland, of course, I've known just about everybody who has operated in letters during the past seventy years. I knew John Buchan who prefaced my first book* and Sir Herbert Grierson –

Buchan must have been the very antithesis of what you stand for.

He was in many ways, and yet he gave me a sympathetic introduction to that first book of Scots lyrics. The man nearest to me, though not so well known as Buchan, was a better writer, R.B. Cunninghame Graham, better known in Latin America than over here. And Compton Mackenzie – I worked with him at the end of the Twenties and have kept in touch since. Like Cunninghame Graham he is a Scottish Nationalist, not quite as I am, but rather Liberal and in favour of Scottish Home Rule, something which to my mind is insufficient. I want complete disjunction from England and a Workers' Republic of Scotland, a different thing altogether, but I've remained on good terms with Compton Mackenzie, as with a host of other Scottish writers like the finest of all in the independent Scottish tradition, the man who wrote under the pseudonym Lewis Grassic Gibbon. He and I collaborated in a book called *Scottish Scene.* I knew him well.

Do you think in the present age small countries are more likely to become conscious of their position and their language?

I think that is decidedly what is happening. We used to be told that any attempt to revive the use of Scots or Gaelic as a literary medium was futile, that the world was moving towards greater internationalism. Burns was told in his day by the Edinburgh literati that if he persisted in writing in Scots he would only reach a small Scottish reading public, but of course he reached a worldwide public. Now this is happening in the case of new, small, independent nations in the last decade or so, and there's no question but that many small countries are going to assert themselves

*Northern Numbers: a selection from living Scots poets (1922)

and demand their independence. The world languages are not, as was anticipated, becoming media. What is happening to the English language, for example in the African countries and elsewhere as those countries regain their independence, is the form of English which they use differs from Standard English even more than Scots differs from Standard English or American colloquial speech differs from Standard English, and I think that difference will persist because, after all, humans are various and their needs and circumstances are various. Each country differs in essential ways and I don't think a common medium is desirable or possible.

Do you feel sad, though, that poetry has such a tiny minority audience? Anywhere in the world it never seems to break through to the masses.

It never has done, and I don't know the answer to that. I don't know why that should be so but it is undoubtedly the case. Yet concurrently with insistence on national liberation, a change is coming over affairs with regard to poetry. I know that in the Soviet Union, for instance, they have a Poetry Week, and during that week all over the vast congeries of Republics, poets read their poetry in local bookshops and in that week hundreds of thousands of copies of contemporary poetry are bought by people; it takes only a few days for an edition of 30,000 or 40,000 to exhaust itself. That hasn't happened yet in this country, but in the last few years there has been a development in and a success of poetry readings in public and over the radio and television. It's difficult in most cities now to attract an audience to a lecture or discussion of any kind. When I was a boy there were mutual improvement societies where people would turn up and argue matters, but that doesn't happen much today, yet whenever there is a poetry reading there is usually an adequate audience, and such readings pay, which I think is the first time one could say that about such recitals. We have a long way to go yet before we can do what they manage to do in Russia when Yevtushenko can get up in the open air and attract an audience of thousands, even on a cold day! Maybe we will come to that one day in this country, too.

What about American poets?

Louis Simpson and Robert Lowell are good, though Lowell I'm not too sympathetic to. Muriel Rukeiser I've known for many years and she seems to me very good.

You never met D.H. Lawrence, did you? I would guess you were unsympathetic to him and his ideas?

I would have been against the Puritanical element in Lawrence, but on the other hand there are things in Lawrence which would have attracted me strongly. I like a lot of his poetry. I'm not particularly interested in his ideas about the blood, a Fascist idea, but he was a great writer. I missed him, and I missed meeting Joyce though I invited him over to a meeting of the P.E.N. club but couldn't get down on that occasion.

Like yourself, Joyce was fascinated by language.

Oh, he influenced me immensely. I was in the happy position of coming across his work very early and he stayed an influence, as the Irish did generally. I was interested in the whole question of the Irish Revival, both on the language side, the Gaelic, and in English.

It's good to think that the Celtic countries are continuing to speak their languages.

Oh yes, especially in Wales where they have hung on to the language. They have hung on to their language very much better than we have in Scotland, and they now publish a lot in Welsh; it's being encouraged. But even in Scotland, there have never been so many learning Scots Gaelic in classes all over the country; there's a real interest. It will come, no doubt.

Are you much involved in Scottish politics now?

I stood against Sir Alec Douglas Home as a Scots Nationalist in the General Election.

How did you get on?

Oh, poorly. It was an impossible aim as we had had no previous candidate or membership in his constituency, which is huge, of course, 8,000 square miles! And they're feudal, large estates with most of the populace estate workers who had never seen a Communist before and expected me to have a bushy beard and a knife between my teeth. But it was useful because the reason we stood was to secure broadcasting time for the minor parties; the Welsh Nationalists had it and the Scottish Nationalists, and so we achieved it too, the Communists. The poll was against us, of course, but that was bound to be.

But you staked your claim.

We did that and we won our point. As one of the judges said in private afterwards, 'It wouldn't have done to unseat Sir Alec Douglas Home.' Well, if that had happened, we'd have unseated Harold Wilson, too!

Is the Scottish Nationalist party divided politically? Your point of view not be shared by other Scottish Nationalists?

The majority of Scottish Nationalists are Liberal. It's growing rapidly and it will come alright, I've no worries about that. This was only the beginning. The really significant thing to have happened recently was at my instigation largely: when the Communist Party of Great Britain was formed, the greatest proletarian leader Scotland ever had was in gaol – John McLean, who didn't want a Communist Party of Great Britain but a Communist Party of Scotland, and he wanted the Scottish Communists to make common cause with the Irish and Welsh, and when the Communist Party of Great Britain was founded, he never joined it. Prior to the 1964 General Election the Scottish Committee of the Communist Party issued a policy for Scotland which conceded all that McLean stood for and that I stand for, and they did that in the teeth of the London executive because the English comrades all objected to this, but we won our point, and we *will* win our point.

Oh yes, we are bound to win our point as far as the Communist Party is concerned. But the economic situation as far as Scotland and England are concerned is a difficult thing to undo, and we have an unparalleled emigration drain from Scotland – we lost over 40,000 last year – continuing rural depopulation, and nothing fundamental is being done about these problems. The Westminster government is directing more and more American firms, which want branch establishments, into Scotland rather than into England, so that we are subsidising the English government and thereby losing fifty million pounds a year.

I wonder if they will ever repopulate those vast areas of the Highlands and Islands?

Difficult to see how they can, except by an incursion of the English. England is overpopulated, relatively, and I've always argued that the ultimate objective of English policy is to use Scotland as Lebensraum. Some years ago we had some agitation in Scotland about an alleged Irish invasion; there was some immigration into Scotland but mainly navvies, manual workers, and they did essential work for Scotland, but what is happening now is an increasing invasion of English and they're not manual workers but white-collar executives, which is a more serious thing. Yes, the huge Highland area could be redeveloped.

There has traditionally been a close connection between Scotland and France, two very different races.

I don't know if that could ever be revived. They have certain things in common: the French are basically a Celtic people, unlike the English and again unlike the English who are inductive, mentally we are a deductive people and so are the French, which is where the French logic comes from. And your surname is French. Oh, you'll have to come back to Scotland where you were born!

Stanley Middleton *(1978)*

I'm talking to Stanley Middleton who began publishing his novels in 1958 with A Short Answer *and has continued to write prolifically since then; this week his nineteenth work of fiction is due to appear.*

You said to me earlier that you thought a novel came about as the result of a challenge. Would you amplify that?

It's a challenge in this sense: any novelist has things to say about life and the problems that interest him, but we were talking about technical problems, and I had in mind the kind of technical problem I set myself in the novel *The Two Brothers* in which I killed off one of the two brothers half way through the book – the brother I liked the better of the two – and then kept him alive in the sense that things happened about him, some of his writings turned up. That sort of problem interested me. I know it has been done before: Julius Caesar dies half way through Shakespeare's play, and he was 'mighty yet' to the end. A technical problem like that intrigues me, time shifts: I read somewhere that their oughtn't to be any flashback in novels, a comment by some idiot critic, so I thought it time I wrote one which consisted mainly of flashbacks. This was *Holiday,* which dealt with three separate lots of time all at once. Again, a reviewer said recently that he wished I would set a novel in the South of France, say, or somewhere other than Nottingham, so I thought I would write a novel set in Nottingham and treat it as a strange land, and that is the one just about to come out called *In A Strange Land* when the people here are mainly not Nottingham people. So it's that kind of technical problem that interests me, but I have to say that it isn't the most important thing.

Incidentally you didn't mention that your novel Holiday *won the Booker Prize, which is a comment on the critic's view! That question of technique does interest some readers: do you find that technique emerges as the result of your engagement with a scene, something that germinates as you work on a specific passage, or is it something you are aware of constantly as you write on, page after page?*

I find that a difficult question to answer because the two are probably the same. My novels grow rather than being written to a plan; perhaps I shouldn't admit it – it makes me sound like an amateur – but when I begin a novel, I haven't any idea how it will end. I begin with some problem, some scene, something very simple, as in a novel called *A Serious Woman;* when I started that book all I knew was that a girl, a schoolteacher, met her father whom she disliked at the top of Friar Lane in Nottingham at the entrance to The Park. That is all I had to start with, not enough for a short story, so that that is an illustration of what is required by technique to make a tale grow out of the scene which you are gradually developing.

It takes me about a year to write a novel and I usually keep to about a year's worth of time, which has advantages: you won't get the flowers in the garden wrong if you are keeping up with time. Things of that sort of … it is not always the case, because in one work called The Wages Of Virtue the time scheme was much longer and concerns a young man who was a conscientious objector in the War, and his life runs roughly parallel to mine though his views were not mine, because I went into the army. Incidentally, if that novel seems to be a good shape – and I haven't heard anyone declare that it isn't – then I might say that I cut out six chapters from the beginning which will still be extant somewhere and haven't been published, and they include a scene which I like very much. So – a sacrifice!

I think my novels are about people in crisis: death, bereavement, changes in personality, change of job, loss of money – and other people intervene, interfere. In the case of The Wages Of Virtue, the boy's mother is a strong woman in her way, intelligent but not educated, and that again presents a technical problem, to show that. She goes along to see the headmaster of the boy's grammar school because he has been wrongly punished, and she gets away with it very well. Now in the early part of the book in the chapters I missed out, she goes to see a singing teacher who is giving her husband lessons. He is a carpenter who has a good voice but on stage becomes very wooden, so the wife interviews the teacher to ask what her husband's chances are. She gets nowhere but has obviously impressed the man so much that he sings the opening of Elijah! I was sorry to have had to scrap that scene, but the fact is that for various reasons, bits that you might have enjoyed have to be scrapped.

Do you explore the crises in families which so often happen in your novels, through dialogue? Is that the way you let people expose themselves, consciously or unconsciously? Obviously you are conscious of it through your art. Is it the main way in which you achieve that effect in your readers' minds?

I think so – I hope it is, though in the novel I'm writing now I feel as I read it through that I'm putting in too much of my own comment on the action, so that finally that may have to go. It may be that I'm changing, possibly even improving, but it will have to be looked into. What is moderately easy for a novelist to do is to describe somebody, to say that this man has these characteristics or that sort of background, but what is difficult is to make a person *act out* what you have said he is. And remember that acting out doesn't mean he acts always in a stereotyped way; there will be some occasions when he will act as we say, 'out of character,' and yet we still have to give the appearance of his real essence – you must avoid being simply irresponsible. At the end of the novel the reader hasn't got to say, 'I don't know what this character is likely to do next!' Sometimes I find this is what I feel when I read the work of some quite distinguished contemporaries, that there has been a sense of irresponsibility. But it is very difficult to make people act as you say they are.

What about pace, actually moving the story along? Does this give you problems or is it now virtually second nature?

I suppose it is, but I wouldn't think that the stories *qua* stories in my novels are of any great interest. It's always been said that you can write the plot of any great novel on a postcard, and in my case I doubt if the story as such is all that interesting. Somebody said to me that he thought *Two Brothers* had more story to it than many of my novels and that it was an advantage; I don't think that was the case, but it was interesting to have an outside opinion. The story is not of particular value to me. I'm not decrying the story, not saying as E.M. Forster said, 'The Story, alas!' but I have to say that I am interested in other things.

Do you have an ideal reader in mind when you write? Or is it something which would paralyse you if you dwelt on it?

The only reader I have in mind is myself. Because I teach, myself, and sort out literary texts with pupils, I can see some of the difficulties, but I don't ever think of an ideal reader; I realise that if a word or a quotation is not picked up by a reader, I am losing something. In *Holiday* I described the death of the hero's very young son, and in the course of the scene in the hospital after the boy has died, I use, unacknowledged, a couple of quotations, disguised quotations, from *King Lear*. Now I would want the reader to pick those up and all that *King Lear* meant, to be added to what I had said, and if the reader failed to pick it up, then I would feel that he is missing something. This is the danger – that a word has, for me, certain powerful echoes which may not have the same echoes for my reader, and that is the difficulty with any sort of writing. You are using words in a peculiar way and you want the reader to run alongside you; I use the word 'run' rather than 'stroll,' as in an afternoon constitutional, because the reader has to work with you. That may be asking a lot but that is really what I want, a reader who will run alongside you, because literature doesn't exist for me unless there is somebody reading it.

Much of your skill lies in the delineating of emotion, of crisis, threats, unresolved ambitions, fluctuating lust, or hope, or fear, centred in the family very often, the family being the source of all our discontents, I suppose. Is that a natural place to start, because it has such central significance to anyone's life?

I would have thought that is the case in our kind of society, though it is not the only place by any means. It is one of the most important places, and that is why I work on it. All these matters of crisis, threats which you mention, I feel are inside myself. When you see me you see a decent, middle-class, middle-aged gentleman, in fair shape, who doesn't look worried, but *inside* me are all these difficulties and dangers. I feel that in some ways I have been very lucky in that I have been able to get rid of such conflicts within myself by writing, which of course says nothing about the literary value of the books; the fact that the books have been therapeutic to me doesn't make them good or bad, but I do feel this element does exist.

In several of your books there is frequent reference to music. Do you have a personal interest in music as a player, a performer?

Yes, I love music. But I play the piano, sometimes the double bass, and also the organ. I often wish to spend more time on music than I do, but I suspect that isn't true – people do what they want to. I'm greatly interested in music.

You mentioned your teaching. You are Head of English at one of Nottingham's grammar schools, and that leads me to ask if you think of this activity as a kind of bridge? Does it complement or supplement your creative work? Is it a support to you as a writer? You must go through set texts for school and university scholarship work, analysing them with your pupils. How does this relate to your work?

Not much. It may seem odd to say this, but I don't often think about my creative processes. As I talk to you or when I give lectures, I have to think about it, but by this stage I have got into habits of writing which mean I simply get on with it and hope to goodness that I'm lucky enough to pay sufficient attention, that I'm not just writing the same old novel again and again.

Certainly the fact that I have to look at literary texts and have done for a long time means that I understand what words are doing; I lay heavy interest on words and am more interested in poetry than in fiction. The thing about teaching is that much of it is boring, having to read essays and setting people on the method of passing examinations, which is what education seems to mean these days. It is a social activity, unlike writing which is a lonely activity: looking at that blank sheet of paper – I wouldn't put my worst enemy to it!

What about writing for television? You said that the writing of television plays has little or no appeal for you.

I am not a great watcher of television so I speak out of ignorance, but I don't feel that such plays can deal seriously or at sufficient length with the things I want to say. Perhaps that is sad, on my part. Did I never tell you about the occasion when I was invited to the Television Centre? I was asked to go and see a producer who said, 'You write very good dialogue. Why don't you think about writing television drama? We are always on the lookout for new writers.' I think they thought my interest had been aroused, because they began to outline the limits of such writing, saying, 'You have to remember that it's family entertainment. And you wouldn't for instance be attacking the Queen, would you? Nor the Church. Nor would you raise the question of homosexuality. And it's quite expensive to make such films, so you wouldn't change the scene too often?' You can tell that all this took place some time ago. So I sketched a little scenario based on their comments and said I would set it in a telephone box with the Archbishop of Canterbury ringing up the Queen about homosexuality! It could go quite well. I think that sums up what I have against that form.

With such high productivity this must betoken that you are a methodical writer?

I would think that I write about 700 words at a sitting. I write in longhand with a fountain pen, not a ball point, though when I wrote radio plays I used a ballpoint because I could get along quicker. That is about my sort of speed and for about five days a week in holidays and three or four when I'm at school. Sometimes the day's work is done in an hour, but

I think better on my feet when I'm walking about, and once a novel is under way I'm thinking about it all the time, not just when at the table, pen in hand. You may be thinking of a scene, worried about something, ideas come quickly, so you work that out on your feet, and I find that next day I can sit down and I know which way it will be tackled; it may, unfortunately, be wrong but you know how to go on. I always like to leave a novel at a spot where I can easily pick it up again. I don't write myself out and then have to restart all over again but rather prefer to leave myself with a bit of something to say.

I also write in hardback exercise books. If I were advising a young novelist, I'd recommend looseleaf books so that changes were easy to make. If I could, I'd write straight on to a typewriter, but I can't. I think there is some superstition attached to novel writing: the late, unfortunate B.S. Johnson always used to start a new novel in his mother's front room because that is where he started his first novel.

What about the contemporary novel? Do novelists writing today interest you enough to want to keep up with their work?

Oh surely, surely. I think the novel in England is of good standard, highly competent, and I think if it is of high standard now, then the next generation is likely to produce some outstanding people from them. It is sometimes urged that our novels are limited, that they consist of only about 220 pages, but this seems to me to be a challenge rather than otherwise. There are authors also, very good writers, who are not published; I see MSS which are just as good as any novels in print, and this makes me think that our novel is strong and that people are bothering to fight to reach a standard, even without being published. Publishers are now a little bolder than they were a few years ago, but it is still very difficult to get a novel published. When I started, I remember reading a letter in the *Spectator* which said that anyone who could get 60,000 words down could get it published, but I had been trying like mad and getting nowhere. But yes, I think the English novel is lively, and while there are some things I dislike about it, I think it in good condition. I think the American novel is also very good: Saul Bellow's *Herzog*, for instance; I believe Bellow had about six tries at it before he finished it. Another one is Brian Moore, an Irish-Canadian-American.

How about established ones like Kingsley Amis, Iris Murdoch, Angus Wilson?

134

Amis I like very much indeed; he's lively, irreverent – a poet, I really think he is a poet, and you can see this in the way he will describe a scene: it's utterly clear in that it's visually grasped, but he has the exact words and that is one of a poet's gifts. Amis I approve of; I didn't think *Jake's Thing* was a great novel but I had a laugh every now and then. Iris Murdoch not so much, because sometimes Iris Murdoch is a bit irresponsible, but she does continue to produce novels and that's what a novelist's job is, not to sit on his or her backside thinking great thoughts, but to be writing novels. Angus Wilson I greatly admired in his earlier novels; I think he has been trying to match the large Victorian novels and the last two I read I did not approve of, *No Laughing Matter* brilliant but trivial, and *As If By Magic* I found myself losing interest in. Still, anyone who has produced one poem or one novel that is good has done something marvellous, and Wilson has done more than that.

Do you ever feel compelled to produce from motives other than from simply wanting to get something down? You don't feel that you have to be writing something out of a fear that you weren't coming up to scratch? Would that be fatal to the imaginative life?

I don't think it would be. I think most writers are compulsive writers, hence I wouldn't feel I was doing my work properly if I were not writing. I would begin to get restless. I also write poems which I make little attempt to get published, perhaps as many as thirty in the last three years. But I think of myself as a writer, I ought to be writing and write I will; I don't think it inhibits the imagination – I don't see why it could. Shakespeare would be asked to write a play or asked to rebuild a play, and Mozart and Haydn and Beethoven would write to order. If it's good enough for those boys it's good enough for me.

Iris Murdoch (1976)

I know you don't like the word 'intuition' when allied to the creative process in novel-writing as an attempt to describe what it is that produces the world of imagination, but you did use the word 'sub-conscious' recently in saying something about the process – that the means by which a writer creates his art may have something to do with the 'subconscious.' I wonder if you could expand on that?

I mean it in the Freudian or quasi-Freudian sense, simply. It is not necessary to go into the scientific question of how exactly the word should be understood in order to decide whether or not such a thing exists. One is aware of a large dark area of one's mind from which all sorts of ideas and images emerge, and certainly in the invention of stories this great abyss can provide unexpected material. There is a well-tried maxim about 'sleeping on it,' when you ask yourself a question at night and find the answer there in the morning. At any rate, when one is tired after trying hard to solve some problem, the answer may come unexpectedly, as if hidden forces had been working on it. I think any artist knows this well, that extra-ordinary imagery and very strange ideas can appear unexpectedly. Think of dreams; here it seems that an extraordinary inventive process is going on of which one knows very little.

I wanted to ask you if you have a switch-on, switch-off sensibility which operates when you sit down to write a novel, but doesn't necessarily need to operate when you write a letter to a friend?

I suspect that most writers, when writing anything, find that whatever it is is permanently switched on. If I write to my bank manager I can't write an ordinary letter to him – I don't know what he thinks about it – but the process of writing is so much a part of the whole being of the person, that one would write letters as a writer does, obviously not with any kind of self-consciousness, but just because the machinery is there and one was using it.

You have written 24 novels since 1954 when Under The Net *was published. Are you ever accused of being too prolific?*

I think it depends on how much energy and imagination one has. I am certainly surprised, looking back at a time when I was doing a full-time job, teaching until 1964, that I still managed to do this work, which of course I could only manage during vacations. Any artist has the problem of how fast he is going to work and when he is to decide when something is finished. I am very meticulous about what I have to do: I always write two drafts, that is, the novel is always written all the way through twice, and many parts are written ten times. The period of primary invention is the hardest and the most important time. Yes, it seems to have come fast, but speaking for myself I don't think it has come too fast.

Your reference to teaching brings me to the next point, the fact that you are a teacher as well as a writer, and also a critic of literature. Does the one in any way impede the other? The fact that half of you has to stand aside objectively and think of literature in a critical sense – does this interfere with the free creative side of you, or do they mutually interact?

I am not a critic and don't write much about literature. I know a certain amount about English literature and I am interested in other languages too, so I have various literary interests, but I'm not a professional critic and I think there is a large difference between somebody who has ideas and someone who is an expert, and I am not an expert.

As far as philosophy is concerned, there is a conflict in terms of time. Philosophy is very difficult and demands one's whole attention too, so that one is in difficulties there. I continue to do philosophy although I'm not teaching it now, but I occasionally give lectures. I would like to write more philosophy. There is always a conflict and this involves one in decisions about how one is going to spend one's time. The activities are totally different. I'm not a philosophical novelist and I don't want the philosophy to get into the novels, since it's a different game, a different way of thinking and a different way of writing.

You have written a book called The Sovereignty Of Good, *a refulgent title with a Richard Baxter feel about it, almost like the work of a great Puritan divine, and you constantly stress that the condition of reality is an unselfed and 'unselving' love. This suggests a religious quality in yourself, although you would question this, I am sure. But I wonder if there is a sense of the religious within your work at its deepest levels, or is it that art is more important to your expression than the explicit experience of religion?*

I wouldn't question your earlier phrase about the religious aspect. I grew up as a Christian. I don't believe the literalistic Christian dogmas any more. But I feel very close to Christianity and to the Christian religion; and I'm interested in religion too, which is a slightly different point. I am very interested in Buddhism, for instance. Yes, there is a religious aspect, and this is something which has increased, perhaps, and about which I have grown more confident, though perhaps not wholly confident. Certainly it is something which has appeared more over my horizon.

The audience for this tape will include librarians, and they will be interested to know how you set about organising your sources of information when you write a novel. Whatever the subject, it requires data, facts about the situation, characters, setting. Do you have a systematic way of garnering the information you may need about people, habits, trivial details?

I often use libraries. I am lucky enough to live in Oxford and I do use the Bodleian if necessary; for instance, for the Irish novel *The Red And The Green*, a historical novel about the Irish rebellion, I spent a considerable amount of time in the Bodleian and this was very rewarding. Of course that is a unique library; there was everything there, all kinds of contemporary pamphlets which I needed to look at, and it was a marvellous experience just to have all this material turning up. One was able to do a good deal of quite minute research easily and reasonably fast, and I have used it for other purposes, too. One should try to get things right.

How do you feel about your audience? You have given a talk with your husband, John Bayley, on 'The Theory and Practice of Novels,' and the question of the 'sharing' of a work with an unseen audience was part of this. Do you feel conscious of your audience at all? Is this necessary or even possible for a novelist?

I don't feel conscious of an audience, no. I think the sharing process happens at a very deep level. It is an interesting and important question, the matter of what, when you are explaining something — and a novel is a great piece of explanation — you take for granted, and what you feel you have to tell. But I think much of this takes place instinctively. It involves the decisions you make about what sort of morality you take for granted and what you feel has got to be invented or put on the table by you, and also, of course, what sort of sheer factual information you assume in your audience. Otherwise, I don't feel particularly conscious of an audience although I'm glad there is an audience! It makes a difference to an artist whether he feels he is showing his work or not: writers in some countries just have to put the stuff away since they know they cannot publish it. Any writer is happier if his material is being offered to an audience, but who the audience consists of, how many there are, or how educated, I don't think bothers me.

What is the difference between a best seller and a serious writer? Is it possible to define this?

Some serious writers are best sellers. I think it's hard to define, and one would have to take individual works and look at them. I think most writers are serious, or at any rate partly serious if they are producing stuff which – although it sounds like tautology – has some pretensions to seriousness. Obviously, there might be pornographic writers or certain kinds of thriller writers who have no object except to produce stuff which will sell; but writing is such a personal business that people invest their thoughts and feelings in what they write, even if they are writing at a popular level.

But when a Harold Robbins produces a number of best sellers, there is somehow a suggestion of the meretricious, that he is calculating his effects and the necessary ingredients in his novels to reach a larger number of readers. Or is this a cynical assessment?

I haven't read anything by him, and I think there are people who do this in a cynical way, but I find it hard to imagine that even if one started off as a cynic, one wouldn't be converted by one's own work.

A question which has troubled me for some time is this: is it possible for the novelist to invent the mimic world that he constructs as a paradigm of the world we live in any longer? Because today the novelist is in competition with films, television, the documentary. Is the old figure of the omniscient novelist able to speak in the same way when he can't even be a specialist? There is such a multiplicity of subjects now requiring specialisation on the one hand, and on the other the journalists. Is the novelist being driven into himself and becoming a more subjective person because of this?

I shouldn't think because of that, exactly. I think he is probably being driven into himself and perhaps becoming more subjective, but I doubt that the proliferation of television and journalistic information really affects the novelist very much because, after all, he is dealing with the great central subjects of human life. Some novelists set up as documentary people themselves and might want to write a novel about the Olympic Games which would be a kind of reportage, and it need not necessarily be a bad novel either, but the ordinary novelist is dealing with the same old subjects, with love and marriage, good and evil, struggling through life and facing death. What kind of particular setting he gives to his novel is no more problematic than it was.

I think there may be general reasons why novelists are now less good. It is indeed a fact that, compared with the nineteenth century giants, contemporary novelists are less good, and quite apart from a sheer lack of talent, this may be to do with a less clear, less confident concept of the individual's relation to his society. This would need a lot of explanation. I haven't in fact got any clear notion why this change has taken place.

I doubt that the novelist is much bothered by the media because he is an egotist and lives in his own world and believes in his own mode of operation and feels separate from all the world of ephemera. It wouldn't for a second occur to me that I was competing with anything except myself and a conception of some of the great people of the past, and even the word 'competition' wouldn't be appropriate.

What would you say you were setting out to achieve by teaching young people philosophy? What is the ultimate value of that particular scheme of education, a degree in philosophy?

At Oxford, philosophy comes in a package, either with politics, economics and some history, or in the classical degree which I did myself, 'Greats,' which includes Greek and Latin language and literature, and Ancient History. I think Greats is a very good degree, a marvellous education because it gives you in its four-year course a tremendous vision of the classical world and of the language, which are useful also in a scholarly sense, and the world of Ancient History, a wonderful world I felt at home in, *a world I identify with,* both the Greek and the Roman classical scene; then philosophy, which begins with Plato and Aristotle and goes on to the present day.

I think philosophy is extremely good training for anyone who wants to do anything. Although that is an idea which people may speak scornfully of now, I think it does teach one to think, it teaches judgement insofar as it can be taught, it gives confidence in dealing with conceptual problems wherever they arise, and of course they arise everywhere. For instance, I was, because of the War, directed immediately after my degree into the Civil Service, and I found that in doing that completely different sort of work, the philosophical training did help. It does clarify the mind, quite apart from the innate interest of a subject in which one is dealing with, the greatest minds of the past struggling with the greatest problems of human life. I was touched to get a letter from an Indian girl who had been a pupil of mine and struggling with great difficulties since she was involved in politics and constantly in debate and argument, and she said, 'I feel like a giant here because I can think much more clearly than most of my opponents.' She attributed this to having studied philosophy.

Does it help to have a deeper moral sense, or not necessarily? Is it a subject laid out, like botany, no more involving of the whole psyche?

I think many people do philosophy without having any idea of its connecting with religion or in a deep sense with morality. This is partly a matter of temperament, and it is hard to say what it is in people that makes them want to reflect about religion or morals. The reasons for this go deep into each individual's life. I believe many are inspired by this aspect of philosophy – I think I was, perhaps not so much when I was an undergraduate, but later on. Contact with great moralists like Kant or Plato can stir and clarify one's imagination and reflection. One can be taught to think about these matters. The finest metaphysicians offer us explanatory pictures of human existence.

A philosopher could use the word 'love' without embarrassment?

That is an interesting question. I think many modern philosophers would feel they should avoid terminology of that sort; they would feel it could not be translated into the kind of philosophical terms they are using. It is a concept which is deliberately excluded by those who create certain types of philosophical terminology, it would suggest to them a religious approach, or they would find it a muddled idea they couldn't use! But after all, love holds a central place in human life, and Plato who founded Western philosophy placed it in his concept of Eros. Platonism passed into Christian theology. Philosophers should turn to these matters. I also believe that it is time for philosophy and theology to attend to each other.

Which brings me to two words that I have seen you use in your books and perhaps I could ask you briefly about them. Somewhere you wrote that your theme is 'transient mortal creatures subject to necessity and chance.' What do you mean by necessity and what do you mean by 'contingency'?

In a sense the two concepts are the same, for what looks like chance in one context is necessity in another. I simply mean the way in which human life so relentlessly forces people into patterns which they have only half chosen, or not chosen. If one thinks of any human life, it is full of irrevocable decisions, paths which diverge, and you are a totally different person if you choose one path from the one you would have been if you had chosen the other path. And there are painful kinds of necessity involved in most people's lives: they have to do a job they don't want to do, they have to live in a place they don't want to live in. Everything to do with family life is full of necessity.

Certain kinds of philosophy – Existentialism, for instance, a philosophy with which I disagree – and certain quasi-philosophical attitudes suggest that human life is full of choices and that in reality one is totally free. I think this is an illusion. Free will operates within a small area. One is surrounded by a causality which one only partially understands; in fact, one can understand very little about one's situation, and this is what it's like to be human. Causality may meet you in the guise of a choice that is forced upon you where you at least see what is happening, or else in the form of an encounter with a motor car in the middle of the road. Chance in that awful sense is always with us.

Is that what Camus was trying to struggle with in L'Etranger (The Outsider)? His hero, Meursault, as someone free of the normal bourgeois choices that bother us? Would you say that novel was successful in that respect?

It is a memorable novel. I'm not sure about what you say since it is complicated by the personality of the chap. Camus wants to present him as a doomed man, doomed by a sort of mad liberation that has come upon him. I think well of the novel but I think there is something murky in the conceiving of it, which is part of its force. It seems to me there is a kind of demonic element involved which isn't anything to do with thoughts about freedom but something in Camus' mind, some deep thing of his own. Meursault looks to us like a man with an obsession, and obsessions obstruct liberty.

When you feel like saying, 'I'm deeply moved by a novel,' what exactly, as far as anyone can be exact about this, would this mean to you? What qualities in it would have that effect on you?

There are good novels of so many different kinds, that is what is so marvellous about the novel, and one is moved in many different ways. I think it is the Shakespearean quality in great novels that moves one – that is an idea I keep coming back to – when a novelist can present a human drama and character in a significant way, and at the same time with great art, often making it very funny, too – the great novel is always funny – in fact, I think the novel is essentially a comic form (tragedy is for the theatre), not meaning by that full of jokes but that it is about the absurd detail of human life, the way in which one cannot fully understand what is happening. Life is muddle and jumble and ends inconclusively, and when this is presented with great comic art, the sorrows of human life can be truthfully conveyed; one is moved by the spectacle and feels that something truthful has been told in a magical way. In Shakespeare you have a dramatic story wherein something quite true, and often intellectually very profound, is contained, completely transmuted into poetry and magic. This is what I think the great novel does, too.

You said you thought Shakespeare was the top novelist.

Yes, I think so. Of course he is not a novelist but he does what novelists ought to be trying to do, and he has the advantage of the magic of poetry, and this makes the whole thing different in a way; yet I think the particular free quality in Shakespeare, the way in which he produces great free characters and yet relates them together and has a pattern which is not an obsessive pattern but a beautiful pattern, a magical pattern in a non-obsessive, free sense – that is what one must attempt to do.

I wonder if we can conclude with one or two questions about writing; for example: what sort of relations have you had with publishers? Have they been agreeable? Are they easy people to deal with, or are they demanding?

I've been lucky. I happened immediately upon two publishers, one English, one American, with whom I've had perfect relations, in fact they are my friends. I think writers do often have difficulties, but it's a matter of luck who you land with. There can be feuds – I know some who are involved in feuds with their publishers, and this is painful and I'm glad that I am not.

Did your first manuscript travel very far before it was accepted – your first novel, Under the Net?

That wasn't by any means the first novel I wrote. I wrote several novels or parts of novels before that, which were very bad, and which I just put away, and one I tried on a publisher who rightly turned it down, and I put that away and tried again. When *Under the Net* came along I did have a certain confidence in that, and the first publisher I offered it to accepted it.

How do you feel about Creative Fellowships in Writing, and Arts Council grants, the kind of encouragement one sees on all sides nowadays – though presumably writers say insufficiently. Is it relevant to what a writer can do or what he's about?

I think a writer would be very unwise to imagine that he can live by writing, and I think that particularly for a young writer it's probably better if he does another job anyway, rather than regarding himself as a dedicated figure, isolated, who somehow has a right to live alone and write. This sounds hard because doing a full-time job and trying to write at the same time is painful, and also of course may be wasteful of a person's talent – it is a difficult point. I would think that writers would be well advised to have an ordinary job, particularly as living on grants is dicey since there's very little money available; I would regard that as an emergency relief operation for artists. There are artists, such as sculptors, who need expensive materials and a grant would enable them to do a big work which they couldn't otherwise do. Writers don't in that sense need material, they need time. I can think of somebody who is a very talented novelist, now trying to complete a work, but with three children she is in all sorts of difficulties from which she could be relieved by some money; even if this helped her for a year it would be a great benefit. I think the Arts Council tries to find out situations of that sort and give emergency relief, and this is an important function.

And Public Lending Right?

Yes. I think that is very important, especially for writers who are not writing but whose books are continually being read.

145

Edgell Rickword (1977)

You were one of the pioneer literary critics of the twentieth century, beginning your life's work just after the First World War. Where did your influences come from and what prompted you to start looking at literature in what was a new way?

I didn't think of it as a new way, but in Colchester I had access to a public library and so to many books which I could never have afforded otherwise, though I also bought books more often than I could really afford. I began to write reviews.

I believe for the New Statesman?

Yes, in 1919, and articles on French writers – Rimbaud, for instance, and I then had an introduction to Bruce Richmond, editor of the *Times Literary Supplement,* an affable and helpful man, helpful to beginners, who gave me a fair amount of reviewing, which kept me afloat. They were paying three guineas a thousand in those days which was more than most papers, and there was *space* in which to spread an argument.

You therefore had a fair degree of experience in reviewing and essay writing before 1925 when you founded the Calendar of Modern Letters?

Many reviews and pieces were in now forgotten journals, not worth preserving.

How did you get the idea of publishing a quite new kind of literary journal?

I suppose every young man wants to found a paper, and I was no exception. I was fortunate in a friend of mine who shared similar literary tastes and thoughts about literature and its development. He was at Cambridge, a student, but when his father died suddenly he decided to quit the degree course and came to London where we met. His closest friend was another Cambridge man whose father was considerably richer than anyone we knew, a big man in the City, named Wishart, later of the publishers Lawrence and Wishart. After a good deal of persuasion he put up the money to start the *Calendar.* I met my co-editor, Douglas Garman, first in 1922, and up at Oxford I met Roy Campbell, a vital person and an influence, though I wasn't necessarily in sympathy with him, but I liked him as a friend. He married one of Garman's sisters which tied things up a bit. Then Edward Muir, the Scottish poet, did some criticism for us on the *Calendar* and he and his wife were translators from the German.

Was it by meeting informally, in conversation, and in other people's homes that you found you had something in common? I am curious as to how this powerful organ of literary criticism started, with the same outlook and voice.

The kernel of it was Douglas Garman, myself, Bertram Higgins and, later, John Holmes. We saw a lot of each other, and we were not all literary journalists. We started the *Calendar* as a monthly for a year, couldn't afford it after that, and it became a quarterly which only survived for six issues. So we were on the scene for about two years and a half, from 1925 to 1927. It was abandoned largely because of lack of sufficient finance, and also there were not enough contributors with novel enough feeling or enough of a strong personal view of the contemporary world to encourage us to go on. They were scattered in different ways: Alec Brown went digging in Central Europe, which didn't allow him to be such a frequent contributor.

Your were interested in the new poets particularly, I think: T.S. Eliot, Ezra Pound, as opposed to the Georgians?

That's true, though I don't think we did anything about Ezra Pound.

You wrote a famous review of The Waste Land *which today reads almost prophetically because the weaknesses you saw in it then have more recently been seen to be present. But to be presented with a poem of that complexity and tackle it as well as you did was quite an achievement.*

Well, I was simply given it to do by the editor of the *TLS* and left with it. I had read Eliot's early poetry, *Prufrock*. I don't know if the review was quite fair to Eliot.

One result of the Calendar *was to influence F.R. Leavis's work, notably his journal* Scrutiny *whose title in fact was adapted from the title of a regular column you ran in the* Calendar *called 'Scrutinies.'*

When we found we couldn't afford to continue the periodical we thought to publish the most original contributions in book form, which we did under that title. I started that column in the first issue with a piece on Sir James Barrie, highly critical, contrary to most views of him.

Oh, he was one of the gods of the period!

Yes, and from that time he has come in for a good deal of criticism. The first edition of 'Scrutinies' went into a second impression, which was unusual for us, and we prepared a *Scrutinies II* to deal with the more contemporary writers than the previous generation. We had a go at Wyndham Lewis, for example.

When in 1932 Leavis's Scrutiny *came out, had you given up literary criticism, looking for other outlets for your writing? It is as if Leavis took over the ideas you had already introduced, rigorous examination of the text, and no reputation sacred.*

Yes, before *Scrutiny* he published with us a little book called *Towards Standards Of Criticism* which gained a big reputation, and in it he paid our work a generous tribute.

As you watched his work developing did you feel he was doing the same sort of thing that your group had been doing?

No, I thought them academic, mostly from the university ethos.

And you saw literary criticism as something that could come from non-specialists?

It could belong to specialists and non-specialists but shouldn't be confined to specialists. There were some good people coming up at Cambridge at that time: William Empson and I.A. Richards. I met Empson soon after he published his first book of poems[1]. A stimulating man, and very different from others of the time; his first book of criticism, *Seven Types Of Ambiguity* was suggestive but very difficult, though the work was a formative influence. I don't think anyone could easily catch up with him in intelligence! A disciple, of course, of I.A. Richards.

You were still writing and publishing poetry yourself in the 1930s?

I published three small collections up to 1930[2].

It's often been said that it's a pity we didn't have more poetry from you.

I would have liked to write more poetry if I'd had the feeling, but I didn't wish to write poetry unless I felt I had to. I was by then reading MSS for Wishart & Co, the publishers, recommending works for publication

[1]*Poems* (1933)
[2]*Behind the Eyes* (1921); *Invocations to Angels* (1928); *Twittingpan* (1931).

including fiction – Ralph Fox, for instance, who wrote novels as well as political works and was killed in the Spanish Civil War.

And with the Thirties we are in the political decade. What were your feelings about the threat that was ever-present in the Thirties from the rise of Nazism? Did you think it time to apply yourself to something more actively political? You went over to the Left Review *at this time.*

Yes, I was one of the founders of *Left Review*. Some people at the time thought that politics and literature shouldn't get mixed up, but it so obviously was.

Many intellectuals turned Left then: the Auden, Spender group, though some might say they were toying with it.

Yes, many of them didn't last long. Spender wrote for *Left Review* and went out to Spain where I met him. I was on a short visit, not there as a combatant, attending a meeting of international writers: Mayakovsky from the Soviet Union, Aragon from France, Ignazio Silone from Italy – in exile by then – and Hemingway from America.

And the young John Cornford and Christopher Caudwell both died in Spain. Did you feel you were living in heroic times?

Yes, I suppose so; exciting, and it made the Second World War more likely. I met George Orwell later, but not in Spain, since he was in Catalonia. An ambiguous figure. His *Animal Farm* was very anti-Soviet. Orwell was very much a loner.

How many years did you edit Left Review?

I was on the editorial board from the beginning and then took over the editorship for a couple of years. After that I lost my job at Lawrence & Wishart so couldn't afford to live in London and went to live in the country which meant I had to give up the editorship. I did a little political writing and some reviewing for the newspapers, the *News Chronicle* was one, but I was generally hard up and living with my wife and my wife's mother near Winchester, and when her mother died went to live in Marlowe on the Thames. There wasn't anywhere to write, but I did an essay on André Malraux for John Lehmann's *New Writing*, Malraux being a significant figure at that time and a prolific writer of fiction and of polemical prose. He did heroic work in the Resistance after the German invasion of France, a real Communist.

Were you able to keep on writing meanwhile?

I neglected to say that during the Second World War we ran a restaurant and after giving up that enterprise opened a boarding house. At that time I also was involved in translating and arranging for translations, a job which became irksome after a time, and I joined the board of a Communist Party paper called *Our Time* which had broader interests than purely Party politics, and I became its editor from 1944–47. I worked with people like Montague Slater and Francis Klingender and enjoyed that experience; it's a paper still well worth looking at.

Coming up to the present time, you have still continued writing, and contributed a long introductory article for the Pelican Guide To English Literature, *soon to be going into a revised edition³. Do you think that Marxist theories of literature are helpful to an understanding of what a novelist or a poet in the central tradition of European literature is doing? Does it help a reader coming fresh to D.H. Lawrence or Eliot or Forster to read the criticism of, say, George Lukacs or yourself in your later phase? Is it too much of a straitjacket to apply to literature?*

I don't think it can be applied just like that. The literature would continue to be what it is if there had never been a Marx! That's not to denigrate Marx, but I don't think he raised the quality of literature. He gave us an insight into the workings of society which the writers will have absorbed and adapt into their own life and work.

And this helps explain the world of, say, Lawrence or Henry James or Valéry – their impression of existing society? This can take us into their world by analysing it from a socio-economic point of view?

I think it helps, yes.

I'm interested in this because I tend to bracket you with the other great critic of our time, Leavis, although I know you say you departed from him, as he was too academic. Leavis, for his part, rejected theoretical Marxist approaches as too rigid, not attending to what was going on in the text.

There was too much rigidity, and Soviet criticism is too mechanical. I don't

³'The Social Setting (1780–1830),' *New Pelican Guide to English Literature*, vol. 5

think the Russians themselves have produced a profounder method of approaching literature. I think it too rigid.

And what is your view of American critics who owe a lot to your work? People like R.P. Blackmur, Allen Tate, John Crowe Ransom. Is their contribution valuable, do you think?

Tate and Crowe Ransom I know and think very good, others I don't know, but of course they had their own world in focus before Marxism became available as a critical approach. There was a rough and ready method in the United States in the 1930s, good, vigorous stuff. And some earlier American writers had seen life from a Marxist social viewpoint even before – Jack London, for instance, and Dreiser. They thought about the social implications behind their plots and characters.

And now in the late 1970s what are your feelings about our established writers, like Lawrence, and those in the canon of tradition? Can you read them with satisfaction, Henry James, Joyce? Do they mean a lot to you now?

There isn't much of Lawrence that I would want to read again. I think basically he did achieve in the 1920s the best that was in him. He is very good in his plays, but in his novels he is too, oh, I think, apocalyptic in his New Mexico novels. But his early plays are good, vital and naturalistic, and *Sons And Lovers.* As to Joyce, yes, the realistic parts of *Ulysses* …

Is Finnegans Wake *too self-indulgent?*

I don't know if it's self-indulgent. I just don't know what to do with it. But *Ulysses*, a brilliant book.

And a young writer starting out to give us his vision of society today – would it matter if the approach was mystical, deeply subjective, like a Malcolm Cowley, or from the four-square realism of Alan Sillitoe? Would you sympathise with one or the other kind, or would you always confront the text first?

I would confront the text first, of course. Sillitoe has a considerable gift for writing; I don't know if it has remained with him. His short stories are very good and his first novel, *Saturday Night And Sunday Morning,* was very promising. I can't touch Iris Murdoch – can't take it, there's so much of a women's college in it. She's too academic.

Do you still keep in touch with writers?

Oh yes, Boris Ford, and David Holbrook, Jack Lindsay – I can't keep pace with him, his output is enormous and how he does it I don't know. He never seems to make any money out of it, since his books don't ever see a second edition; his books on painters are very good, but he has a wide range of interests.

And what would your message be for a young novelist today?

I'd say, 'You will see much more of the world than we could fifty years ago, and you have much more information – you know how it works. There is so much fluidity about the world now that we don't know when the cauldron will overflow.' The political situation is grim, don't you think? That's something to remember. And the great uncertainties of the present time. The great invasions from the East in the past were pretty terrible but they didn't destroy anything that couldn't be rebuilt. But with the atomic bomb, there is uncertainty. All this is challenging for the creative mind – and you might have to reckon that you could not finish the book! But then artists in the past have in some cases been unable to finish their pictures!

Alan Sillitoe *(1965)*

"Once a rebel always a rebel – you can't help being one, you can't deny that. And it's best to be a rebel and to show them it don't pay to try to do you down. Factories and labour exchanges and insurance offices keep us alive and kicking, so they say, but they're booby traps; they'll suck you under like sinking sands if you aren't careful. Factories sweat you to death, labour exchanges talk you to death, insurance and income tax offices milk money from your wage packet and rob you to death. And if you're still left with a tiny bit of light in your guts after all this boggering about, the army calls you up and you get shot to death. And if you're clever enough to stay out of the army you get bombed to death. Aye, by God it's a hard life if you don't weaken, if you don't stop that bastard government from grinding your face in the muck, though there ain't much you can do about it unless you start making dynamite to blow their four-eyed clocks to bits. They shout at you from soap boxes, 'Vote for me, and This and That!' but it amounts to the same thing in the end whatever you vote for because it's the government which puts stamps all over your fizzog until you don't see a hand before you, and what's more makes you buy 'em so that they can keep on doing it. They've got you by the guts, by backbone and skull until they think you'll come whenever you whistle.

But listen! This lathe is my everlasting pal because it gets me thinking, and that's their big mistake because I know I'm not the only one. One day they'll bark and we won't run into a pen like sheep. One day they'll flash their lamps and clap their hands and say, 'Come on lads, line up and get your money! We won't let you starve,' but maybe some of us will *want* to starve and that will be where the trouble will start. Perhaps some will learn to play football or go fishing up Grantham Cut. That big fat-bellied Union ponce will ask us not to muck things up; Sir Harold Bladdertab will promise us a bigger bonus when things get put straight; Chief Inspector Popcorn will say, 'Let's have no trouble! No hanging around the gates there!' Blokes in suits and bowler hats will say, 'These chaps have got their television sets, enough to live on, council houses, beer and pools, some have even got cars. We've made them happy – what's wrong? Is that a machine gun I hear or a car backfiring? *Tat-a-tat-a-tat-a-tat!* I hope I'm not here to see it, but I think I might be. I'm a bloody billygoat trying to screw the world, and no wonder I am because it's trying to do the same to me."

That passage from Saturday Night And Sunday Morning, *read by Alan Sillitoe, prefaces a short conversation about his work. I'll begin by asking him if he finds writing a solitary occupation or if it opens doors into a new world, a populous world that the artist feels?*

If it opens any doors at all it opens them into myself and not in any exterior world. The exterior world has always been there for me; it might now become a little clearer, a little more comprehensible, but it still has no scheme, no order to it, even though it might change its colour.

Would you say that the production of work is a search for order, for a focus?

Yes, I think that is why, principally, one begins as an artist, and I think I'll flatter myself even at this stage by calling myself an artist. One comes into the world and everything is chaos, and as the child grows up, some sort of order is imposed upon him, but if you have anything of the artist about you, you begin to feel that something is wrong with this kind of order and so you become an idealist and therefore you begin to write. It's difficult because you have to be careful not to let the idealist get a grip on you too much, otherwise it might inhibit you in writing; you still have to retain a sort of naive view of the chaos in order to project something that will have some sort of reality. At the same time, when you write you have to be completely ice-cold.

Does this mean that you mustn't confuse what you yourself feel might be an answer to social or political problems with what you feel as a literary writer you have to do in terms of a novel? Your philosophy has to be kept back or built into your fiction as an integrated part?

Yes. As to political questions, I believe that if there's an insistence on dividing people between Left and Right in politics, then – one is born either Left Wing or Right Wing, part of your character that you don't need to tamper with. Whenever you write, obviously you don't think about politics; you write out of the spring of yourself, and then whatever people say about it they say about it, but at least they can't say that you were not being true to yourself, and that is the prime point, to be true to yourself. You just write from this central point which has no name, and if it had, I wouldn't be talking this way now; that point which is indescribable and has no name.

What did you first feel when you decided, if you decided as coldly as that, to be a writer? Or did you begin writing and then it gripped you to the extent that you had to go on doing it?

Difficult to say. All decisions are made, you discover, only by looking back at them, at least that's how it is with me. I was in Malaya with the RAF and writing a few poems which of course weren't poems, but I thought they were at that time, and then I had to go into hospital and be inside there for about eighteen months – I imagine that often happens to a person who is in gaol or in hospital or a prison camp for a long spell, and then he begins to find out what is really in the middle of himself, or he begins to find out what is there to be tapped, even though he's not quite conscious of it or couldn't explain it.

When I was in the hospital I began to read and at the same time I began to write. I was 20 years of age and I had hardly *read* a book up to then, never mind written one, and then I went back to Nottingham when I was 21 and wrote a novel which has since been destroyed. I used to go into the Reference Library in Nottingham Central Library and sit there and write, my second book which is now in the ice box. After that, writing began to seem to me to be one possible way of living on this earth, a matter of living or dying. When I was diagnosed at the beginning I was told, 'You have tuberculosis,' a blow, like being hit on the head with a hammer, and if I hadn't started to read and write, I probably wouldn't have got over the shock – I could put it as simply as that. It was a gate through which I went, and in any case for three months I was absolutely stunned, perhaps more than I need have been, but nevertheless that's how it appeared to me. Almost a death sentence. So writing had something to do with the shock. In a lesser way it was like someone saying, 'You're to be put up against a wall and shot,' and then suddenly you're not, but the flash in the heart at that moment maybe does something to you. It was rather like that. I'm overdramatising but only in order to explain it.

What did you read, initially?

For some reason I was fascinated by the Greek and Latin authors, and read them all in translation many times, Greek and Latin mythology. In fact that was practically the only thing I read while in hospital. Fortunately, at that time the Penguin Classics were coming out and I read them, and others found in second hand bookshops. I think the first significant writers I read were in France and Spain where I went to live after recuperating: Joseph Conrad, Fielding – and I read through the Bible and Shakespeare! My father had a book called *A Treasury Of Yiddish Stories,* a big, fat anthology which to my view contained some of the most marvellous writing I had seen, especially in the short story form. The way of telling a short story by Israel Joshua Singer and Shalom Aleichem is to begin with a rich language, then turn off at an angle and return again to the central theme and wind around again, with flashbacks; eventually they would get to the end of the story, but it was like hearing a story told around a camp fire by a very old man. These tales seemed to me to be the most perfect stories; they antedated Chekhov and you could see where many of the Russian writers had got their style, or where the famous Yiddish writers had got theirs. To me, the Yiddish stories were much more fascinating because they had dealt with people who were desperately poor and often persecuted, yet with a great sense of humour and immensely alive, and something which seemed to connect up with a spring inside me. I wouldn't go so far as to link the Jewish people of the Stettel with the people of Radford, Nottingham, yet there is some connecting spark to which I responded, and apart from that, the fantastic and beautiful style of the stories appealed to me, and in my own stories I was influenced by these examples. I used the technique in *The Loneliness Of The Long-Distance Runner,* the winding method of narration.

As you read, were you noticing technique, how things were shaped and created?

Not for a long time. I enjoyed them too much to be thinking about the technique. I had written eight or nine novels by then which will never come out of course, but it was by writing that I learned to write, and after about the seventh or eighth manuscript I perceived that I was actually doing things wrongly, and I began to relate them not only to the books I'd read but also to the voice inside myself that wanted to speak, and the more I wrote the nearer the material edged towards the centre line of my own voice, and eventually it clicked. It was then that I began *Saturday Night And Sunday Morning.* There were two novels before *Saturday Night* which I think could have been published, pretty nearly on centre, but they were not accepted and I didn't continue sending them around.

Nottingham is central to your fiction, inevitably because it gave you your background and a way of feeling and thinking. Will it continue to be? Do you think for your own purposes it need be any longer?

I think a writer ideally should write about all kinds of people in any part of the world with which he comes into contact. The reason I began with Nottingham and the reason it figures so prominently in my work is that it took me a long time to establish the fact that you had to write about what you knew. All those wasted manuscripts were about something I didn't quite know, therefore I veered on to this track of writing about what I knew. Now I do know much more, but in ways of change and development I work at my own speed which may seem rather slow but when viewed from the whole extent of a writer's life it might not appear to be slow. If in thirty years' time I look back on this moment, it will be immersed in a gradual flow of development.

You have said recently that poetry means, if anything, more to you than fiction.

I say this but I won't be able to say whether or not it's true for another thirty years! I'd like to say it was true but really one is a writer, novels, short stories, poems, and one hasn't any business to pronounce on which is the most fancied. I think poetry is a better form because you can't write a poem until completely 'inspired' to do so; you can write a novel or short story under a state of semi-inspiration which has a sort of iciness to it in order to get it down completely, but with a poem the iciness doesn't exist, the bitter cold which makes everything clear. It's down, out of the fire, and then you bring your skill to bear to work on it, and if you revise a poem you have to go back, recall that inspiration that led you to write it in the first place. A poem is something almost holy, 'inspired,' so I'm more inclined to say that I like poetry than fiction, in that I find it worth more, but only from that point of view. It's, shall we say, 'divine,' if that word can be used.

Have you any sense at all of compulsion, an obligation to get on with it, now that you are established, or are you quite at ease waiting until your next production properly emerges?

It took me about ten years to be published. I don't think that it is necessarily an immense amount of time, but during the ten years I spent six years out in the wilderness, and in fact abroad, trying to decide in my own wilderness how to do it and what to do. I have no compulsion, because having taken so long to get started, I've a certain amount of iron in my soul and that says to me, 'Go your own way, don't be afraid of anything, take no notice of anyone. You're quite alone and no one can influence you, so sit where you are and work at your own speed and carry on until things come to you. If they come to you, fine, and if they don't, it doesn't matter, there's plenty of time.' That's the way I work. I don't worry.

Are you importuned much for work? People asking you for stuff? Is it part of a writer's lot to expect this through the post?

Yes, a fair amount, and I ignore it because I never write anything to order. If I was asked to write an article on something, I would very politely refuse; if I was asked for a story and had one, I'd let them see it; if I don't have one, I say I'm sorry. I can't afford to produce on demand because my time has to be my own.

Reverting to the Nottingham scene: how about the Nottingham character? Is there anything about it which strikes you as individual, as opposed to other characters you have come across since? Is there an identity about the city quite apart from the fact that you know it well?

I don't think I can claim too much for Nottingham. I wonder if I had been born and brought up in, say, Bristol, I fancy I would have dealt with life in much the same way. Nottingham seems to me to be a lively place – I'm trying to be objective about this – but after having seen most cities in Britain, it does seem to have a spark that most of them don't have. I have to be careful because maybe I'm prejudiced! But it does strike me as a particularly lively city.

Can I ask you about your present reading? Do you bother to keep up with your contemporaries, your fellow novelists, or is it not important to you?

No, it isn't. I read a novel if I think I might like it but I don't 'keep up' because there's nothing to keep up. Keeping up is a mug's game since things worth keeping up with appear so slowly, only once in five or ten years does a book come out which must be read, not in a 'keeping up' way. It is rare. One can be bombarded with all sorts of books but they don't mean much.

You did meet Robert Graves earlier in your life. Was he an influence – was it a happy encounter?

I was in Majorca in the spring of 1953 writing poems and I sent him some over. He was in a village seven miles away[1] and invited me to visit him for tea, so I rented a bicycle for about sixpence and rode over a mountain. We got on quite well – he's still a good friend of mine, comes to see us when he's in England, and last year lent us a house for three months in Majorca.

Now, he comes from a completely different world.

But he's a poet, and yes, though he's from a completely different world, he is also a poet, and so there is meeting ground.

On mythology he is an authority!

Exactly; we talked a lot about that. He was a great help in this way: at that time he wasn't quite the international figure he has since become, and was a living example of how to survive in exile not caring about anyone. He was there in his house and didn't give a fuck for anybody. One had that sort of vision of him carrying it off and hoped it was possible to do the same. I would still have done it, but it was good to know another person had brought it off. At one point we were desperately broke, so he got me some translation work which saved us for a time, some translations from Spanish and French.

You are a bit of a linguist then?

Well, I lived in France for a year and Spain for five years – Majorca – so … what can you do! I also translated from Majorcine dialect.

The threat from anyone in a literary milieu must be constant and insidious, from the lions, the people who want to stalk you, the people who want you to belong to various enterprises, and apart from that, the Metropolitan set. This must be something you have to fight, or can you easily shrug it off?

I find it easy because of that ten years when, as I say, I put some iron into my soul. Without being rude I say, 'I'm sorry. We're busy.' After you have refused fifty or sixty letters they stop pestering you, and you can get on with your work. Having spent those winters in Majorca when we were isolated, without a radio, television, newspapers, books, nothing and no connection with the English literary world. Mostly my influences come

[1]Deya, on the north coast.

from America, strangely enough, from Americans passing through. Ruth (Fainlight) was there with me and I would sit in the room with her reading. We read to each other – I remember reading *Confessions Of An English Opium Eater* and she read the *Gothic Tales* – this instead of having a radio, and that gave us a bit of style. And so we survived.

Would you like to end by reading a poem of yours which you like?

I'll read this one. It's called 'Strategy and Statement.'[2]

> You think: "Be cunning, act the fool,
> Say, "I am not a poet
> But the gods' fool,"
> And then one day
> If any god should want his say
> I'll cut his bollocks off
> And eat them cold,
> Bury myself alive
> Beneath his heaps of gold.
>
> You think so?
> Leave it be;
> Fools' gold, strategy and strength.
> Put all your ironies in one fire,
> Walk the root-marks from your feet
> Until the train is plain behind;
> Do not go forward until the road is empty,
> Move unimpeded to create the best —
> No battles can be won with less than death.

---

[2]Collected in *A Falling Out Of Love* (1964)

Geoffrey Trease (1966)

Geoffrey Trease is a Nottingham author of boys' stories, and I'll begin by asking him about his early days.

I was born in 13 Chaucer Street, just behind the Central Library. I think it has since vanished and I have no recollection of living there because we left after a few months and moved nearby to 142 Portland Road which is the house I remember, near the Arboretum, the public park. It was only five minutes' walk from Nottingham High School where I was educated, walking up the hill to the sound of the school bell which in those days used to ring every morning! My father was a wine merchant with a business in the centre of the city where the family still carry it on, and all my early memories up until the First World War and on until 1928 are of Nottingham. Then, in one respect unfortunately, I ceased to live in Nottingham and went up to Oxford and never came back to live permanently there, though never a year goes by without my visiting the city on family visits or public occasions. I do value the connection and think of myself as a Nottingham man.

What did you read at Oxford?

Oh, I read classics and got so bored after a year that I resigned my scholarship and cleared out. I was nobbled for classics at the High School as a 13-year old boy when my heart was in history, and so I never learned another line of history other than ancient history, which was a great sorrow to me, so since then I've been entirely self-educated historically.

When you left Oxford you obviously had to make a quick decision?

I went to work as a social worker at a Settlement in Bow, in the East End of London, which helped me to sort out my ideas, then found a humble niche in London journalism for two or three years until I married on my 24th birthday and lived ever afterwards in the provinces as a full-time author.

Did you initially decide to write for young people, or was the idea to write in general terms, either adult or youth?

Very much the latter. I meant to be a writer ever since I can remember, and scribbled away as a child, muttering my stories under my breath, and then started little magazines of my own. Through my school career I did a first-form magazine, then the school magazine – I followed the present Dean of Westminster Abbey as co-editor of the school magazine, and the co-editor of my first year was Kenneth Adam of the BBC, so I look back on those early years with considerable interest, the writing and editorial experience. You mentioned boys, but I write for young people, and quite as much for girls and have possibly more girl readers, I don't know. That was almost accidental, I was trying various forms, and that one seemed to be successful, and I've kept hard at that vein ever since, but I am interested in doing the occasional novel when I can or a general non-fiction work. It's not that I'm solely interested in children's writing, but it's the thing that publishers are always wanting me to do.

What kinds of non-fiction works have you done?

I suppose my *magnum opus,* if I can dignify it with such a grand term, was a general history of Italy for adults,* something which I felt nobody had done, beginning with the earliest times. I spent a lot of time on that and was happy doing it, making many journeys to Italy. Another one was a survey of children's literature, *Tales Out Of School,* which I feel to have been an important part of my writing life.

Will you decide upon a theme, a period or person, and then do the homework?

I do most of the homework while writing, but there are always other matters which come to light and that usually entails rewriting, for example I set an action on one particular date in history, the day itself I described as a wet morning when in fact I discovered it was a fine morning, and the whole chapter had to be rewritten. I normally set to work by covering pages and pages of notes, make any journeys I have to make, get the theme clear in my mind before I dare start, because the whole shape of the story could be twisted by an unlucky discovery when it is largely written.

Travel? That's interesting. How far have you had to travel? All over Europe?

I choose my subjects so that Europe will figure in them – I don't tend to set plots in Bolivia – and I like Europe for travel; I've been to Norway, Greece, Italy and, last year, Spain and Portugal in connection with the job I'm doing now.

*The Italian Story (1963)

Do you have any age group in mind as an audience?

I used to, but I found it was hopeless, eventually. I used to think of myself as an author for the eleven pluses, but I now find that the modern, fairly sophisticated child, if it's fond of books at all, can read my stuff from about eight or nine, and my oldest regular reader was the late Sir Charles Trevelyan who was reading them until he was 86! So to cater for specific age groups is impossible, and then again there are foreign children and one doesn't know exactly what they are like as your readers, but I have found that the same book goes down well with Japanese or Sicilian children, so it's much better to write what you feel impelled to write and hope for the best.

Yes, you have been translated into many languages.

The last count was eighteen.

Are there any models after whom you have shaped yourself in this field? I'm thinking of people like R.L. Stevenson. Have they meant anything to you consciously?

I must have been influenced by them, but I don't think I ever consciously had a model. I began to write for children in reaction against the older children's books, more against their values and historical interpretations. I started off writing vaguely like Henty but from an opposite point of view.

The Henty generation was full of imperialist glory and blood and thunder, with titles like Facing Death; *heroes in impossible situations who were thinly disguised empire builders.*

Indeed – though they weren't very thinly disguised! I think the question of violence and danger is a legitimate interest, though it's difficult to be dogmatic about this, and is one which absorbs young people, but I do think it matters how it is presented and interpreted. I don't shy away from necessary fighting and violence, whereas the older generation, living in a more peaceful setting themselves, did not question this so radically. There was too easy acceptance of the glory of war, but for the past thirty years one has not wanted to write adventure stories suggesting that war is glorious or fun. Violence must be recognised both in history and in present day work.

You therefore attempt to render a situation as fairly and squarely as you can, from the evidence?

Yes. I do feel that is terribly important now. I started life as, I suppose, an angry young man in violent reaction against the old standards and I leant to the other extreme, and looking back on my early work I see how propagandist it was. Since then I have realised that the children's writer is like that of a schoolmaster in front of a class; he may have his own views but he has to play fair in dealing with those who have less experience than himself, and he has to present both sides to them so that they can make up their own minds.

What sort of reaction do you get through the post from your readers?

Very interesting. I get a lot of letters from all over the world, particularly England and America. Children write in making comments, some ask for more, some ask searching questions, one presented me with a questionnaire of fourteen questions including, 'How did you meet your wife?' and what was my favourite food? I don't answer all letters quite as fully as the correspondents demand but it is a great joy to receive them.

Do you read your work to audiences?

Very seldom. I do give talks but, except possibly for the sake of illustration when I might read a passage, I don't otherwise give readings.

Have you views about standards in children's writing today? Apart from the question of values. What about the technique, the composition?

My view is that obviously it should be as good as one can make it, both from a literary point of view and the content. I think it a pity that we don't remember sufficiently that a children's writer can be an artist, even though only a minor artist, and certainly there has been an encouraging improvement both in literary standards and in standards of historical accuracy, and there has been an advance in imaginative ideas. I have just been revising that survey of children's literature, *Tales Out Of School,* which first appeared about fifteen years ago, and preparing the new edition I found things had improved so much and that so many of my old criticisms had been satisfied, I had to make almost a new book. In the field of historical writing a whole new school of very fine authors has appeared, like Rosemary Sutcliffe and others, and many of my criticisms in detail no longer apply.

Due to rising standards of education generally?

It's due to many things, among them the fact that the adult novel has gone through a poor period, the children's book has come up in economic terms, in selling value, and now some eminent writers are glad to write children's books because they can't live by their novels. That is quite a factor, I believe.

Librarians are often saddened by the fact that they lose their readers at about the age of 16 and don't recover them until much later. What have you to say about that?

I have heard that and I can very well believe it. There are obviously all sorts of other factors, other preoccupations which press upon them in those intervening years, and it's understandable if their general reading suffers, because even the bookish types are concerned with textbooks, but there does remain a real problem and that is that there used to be too sharp a gap between the end of a children's book with its complete lack of emotional or sexual interest, and the novel intended for older readers. Today, in their rising sophistication, children tend to dismiss the conventional story as kid's stuff. But on the adult shelves they are confronted with the contemporary novel which, I must say in my prejudiced way, has never been more pessimistic and distressing for the young reader. Children then say of that kind of novel, 'This isn't for us, but for a lot of jaded people of thirty-plus,' and that may be the reason for them losing the habit of reading literature. Let's hope librarians can get them back! It will need a lot of work from us authors and I think we have a responsibility to present a picture of the world which will genuinely appeal to the person of sixteen, but not yet disillusioned.

And what are you working on now?

At the moment I'm doing another of what I call my junior historical novels. It will be called *The Red Towers Of Granada* and ends in Moorish Spain but starts in Nottingham in 1290 when Edward I was in the city just before he banished the Jews from England. This means I've had to research into Nottingham history more than I have ever done; my hero starts off by staying in a Jew's house in the ghetto – which turns out to be almost the exact spot where my family have had their wine business for many years, and I've been able to bring in Mortimer's Hole, the cave entrance in Nottingham Castle, and any more I could find in the histories of Nottingham. The first half of the book will be a Nottingham book. The ghetto area, according to Wood's *History of Nottingham*, or possibly it was in Duncan Gray's history of the city, was bounded by Castlegate, Listergate and Houndsgate, and the spot I mention is at the foot of Castlegate.

As to the theme of the novel, I suppose it is toleration. There are Jewish characters and Gentiles and Muslims and it's an attempt to make a link, I suppose, between the twentieth century when the children will know that dreadful things were done, and the thirteenth century when equally intolerant action took place in England.

You said you had got your date from your brother's researches into his angle on history – pharmacology? He is Professor of Pharmacology here at Nottingham.

Yes. In something he had written on his researches into the history of the Royal Apothecaries, I noticed an item which reminded me that Edward I and his Queen had been in Nottingham from September to November, 1290. I wanted to use Nottingham as a setting and it all tied in nicely with the time of the expulsion of the Jews. I also wanted my Gentile character to go to Spain with the Jew who had befriended him, so often that is the way these coincidences work out when you are planning a story, and how a story gets shaped by preparatory work.

John Wain (1975)

We are here at Rhosgadfan near Caernarvon on a glorious day, and our previous conversation suggested many lines. Perhaps I can start by asking an obvious question – the phrase is bound to come up, so forgive me for asking – about the Angry Young Men. You must have as good a claim as any for being the founder of the school with your first novel Hurry On Down *in 1953?*

The realisation that there was an idiom of the Fifties which was not that of the Forties or Thirties broke over people, I think it's true to say, with the arrival of *Hurry On Down*. I started to write it in 1949, on Sundays until by about 1952 I decided I had better get on with it and finish it. But most labels are absurd and are chosen by people who have no fine perception of the realities of the situation. Most labels are ridiculous, even established ones like Romantic and Classic are too clumsy and all–inclusive to be worth anything and yet one uses them because they do signify something. There was a period when one realised there was a Fifties style but it wasn't clear what to call it, and in poetry it was called The Movement, a deliberately meaningless name; nobody knew where to or where from but there was something, and that was what it came to be called. When after the success of *Look Back In Anger,* John Osborne's play in 1956, they looked for something to link it all together, found the old Movement, and called the whole thing the Angry Young Men. I suppose all young men are angry, and if they're not they should be, and all young writers are impatient of their elders and the way the world is, and are stark and hostile, and if they're not they ought to be. So we were, just as the young writers of the Thirties were, like Orwell, angrier than we ever were, but I suppose the Zeitgeist of the Fifties was expressed first in *Hurry On Down* – that seems to be the general feeling.

Looking back at it from the perspective of twenty years later it does seem to me that the Fifties was a period of tranquillity. It seemed as if the major problems were solved; Harold Macmillan could get up and say, 'You never had it so good,' and it was true that wages were higher, the standard of living was higher, international tensions had died down, and it looked for a few years as if prosperity and even peace were here. Then at that very moment a group of writers arose who didn't know one another, working independently, published novels and plays of discontent, impatience, satirical of established manners; like Kingsley Amis they were ironic and quizzical, or tirades like Osborne's work. They were sharp, hostile, and anger seemed to be the tone. Now, years later we can see that all the problems we have now were there under the skin, all the causes of tension, the frustrations, were there then despite temporary lulls. And if the imagination means anything it means that it can divine what is under the surface, so that it seems to me that looking back – we were right. We were getting some kind of seismic signal and our diagnosis of life in the Fifties was actually better than that of the politicians.

You were still at that time a lecturer at Reading University.

Yes, I started as an academic after taking my degree at Oxford and being awarded a Fellowship at St John's College. I was happy in the English Department at Reading, very comfortable, but should have left sooner than I did because by about 1951 I decided that I really wanted to be an imaginative writer and not give my life to the interpretation of other peoples' work, however fascinating that is.

And that was a bold thing to do, to commit yourself to your own potential, your own powers.

Yes, it meant setting out on the wide sea of life with one's own little paddle rather than going in a liner, but at that age one makes bold decisions and thank God I did! I've always been interested in criticism and take great pleasure in classical English literature, I've written a book on Shakespeare and have done books of critical essays since the year when I gave up university teaching. In a curious way it met full circle last year when I was elected Professor of Poetry at Oxford, a post which is not purely academic but is given to a practising poet who has usually some sense of the tradition. So perhaps then my academic life suddenly leapt up out of its grave and for five years now I have this very amicable relationship during which I'm not expected to do any academic work except give some lectures, which simply means standing up and telling people my thoughts – which I'm glad to do. So that early decision has worked out well. I think the way things are now, the serious writer is going to have more of a relationship with the academy than he once did.

Why do you think this is?

Not altogether for good reasons. In a perfectly ordered world it probably wouldn't be true, but in this present world it is --

Economic reasons?

Not altogether – it's to do with the institutionalisation of literature. There was a time – and on the whole I think it was a better time – when the universities existed to teach the classics, Greek and Latin and Medieval and Renaissance literature, and our classics, Shakespeare, Milton and the rest. The modern writer, that is anyone within the past century, was left to the common reader who took an interest in certain writers – it was an agreed system. If those writers persisted to a second and third generation then they were acclaimed classics and would be taken up by the academic establishment, put on syllabuses, lectured on. Nowadays we have phased out that common reader; if a writer produces a book that is felt to be important, within the next few months he can be brought into the academic syllabus, and in a way I think that is sad because it means that the common reader, the person who read simply for pleasure and personal enrichment, who talked about his reading to his friends, lent his books, has been bypassed. They were invaluable, but unfortunately that is so. Since one lives in the real world, one has to accept it. In my own case, I discover that I am a set book in France. Every French student at a certain stage has to read *Hurry On Down,* and whenever I am in France I meet kids with the Penguin edition coming up to me to sign it, not because I am a great writer – they wouldn't know what a great writer was – but because they have to study it at school. So we go along with all that, as we do with a lot of things, the atom bomb, the weather. Weak as it may be, we go along with it.

What did you like best about lecturing at Reading University?

It was a small university then, with just a thousand students and a hundred teachers. I was there the other day and I believe there are now something like twelve thousand students and twelve hundred teachers. In my day it was famed for its Agricultural Department, and there were just a few students doing philosophy, pure sciences and the humanities – it was a very pleasant life. The physical surroundings were agreeable, we didn't have a lot of teaching, and it was all extremely civilised. When I went there as a young lecturer I had about four hours' teaching in a week and the rest of the time I was supposed to improve my mind. I will add that my salary was £400 a year which doesn't sound like a salary at all today. Pleasant students, only four hours' teaching, an invaluable breathing space which I can't praise too highly. I was surrounded by good colleagues who told me what to read, learned men who educated me. My education at Oxford was just the beginning, but in the ten years I spent at Reading I had fellow teachers like Frank Kermode who was in the next room to me; the number of ideas I had from him was incredible. It was a good period but I began to realise towards the end that if I went on much longer I would be taking my salary under false pretences because I wasn't really interested in teaching. After my first novel came out and attracted some attention, I realised I could probably make a career out of writing, and the day I was convinced of that I gave in my notice.

Living In The Present, *your second novel, was in the same vein as* Hurry On Down?

Yes, though I soon saw that it wasn't good enough. I wrote it in the aftermath of *Hurry On Down,* all within a few months, when my publishers said, 'Come now, write another novel quickly or the public will forget you.' So I wrote another novel and realised after its publication that I had made a mistake, and I have taken every opportunity since then to say I don't feel it was a good book. When the paperback edition came out in America I was asked to write a preface, and I expressed certain doubts about the book, and that must be the only case in the world in which a book has an introduction by the author saying it's no good! I know that in a lifetime of writing one will publish some things that do not work, so why not admit that this was one such example and I know it, too.

One of the features of your work which warms me to it is your interest in jazz. It seems to be a mark of our generation. Philip Larkin and Kingsley Amis both share that interest, and your novel Strike The Father Dead *is about a jazz musician wherein you make the distinction between what we all used to condemn as 'commercial' popular music and true jazz, and you seize the opportunity to damn the new and insidious brand called 'pop,' which in 1960 when you were writing the novel, was beginning to conquer the music scene. Since then you have other views on jazz and pop?*

I think jazz is a wonderful art that *may* survive, I don't know. It looked at one time as if it would be as extinct as ragtime. The kind of jazz I admired was played by musicians who were virtuosi, who could play their instruments as well anyone in a symphony orchestra and who were fine artists, and that kind of jazz lasted from about 1915 to about 1960. At the time I wrote that novel, I thought it was going to be engulfed by rock and pop which, whatever their good points, are not the music of virtuosi musicians. Such players are barely musicians at all, like film stars they exploit their own personalities, but the jazz musician is a great artist. Oddly enough, at this moment ragtime is suddenly popular again, so what of my prophecy? Joshua Rifkin is making Scott Joplin's rags sell more than the Beatles. But yes, most of my generation of poets and writers have a deep feeling for traditional jazz, and why not? Philip Larkin's collected jazz criticism, *All What Jazz,* is a superb example, as is his poem on Sidney Bechet, and perhaps I can mention my poem to Bill Coleman, the black American trumpeter who spent most of his career in France, in my *Letters To Five Artists,* which has some of that feeling in it. The portrait of a black jazz musician in *Strike The Father Dead* is based on the same feelings of admiration for this kind of music.

That was the start of a most interesting experience: I had always admired the trumpet playing of Bill Coleman and since I was about 15 in 1945, I had records of Bill Coleman. Years passed and this got buried and I wrote this novel about an English boy, son of a classics professor, who goes off to be a jazz musician and I called him Coleman. Now it's beyond the wit of man to invent a name; nobody invents a name, it rather comes out of memory. I wanted a very English name and I was really thinking of Coleman's mustard, but the fact that I called him Coleman must have deep roots somewhere. I had a mental picture of a black musician who goes to Paris and stays there, and my character wasn't a very skilfully drawn picture but never mind, it was there, and it was a reality in the book. When that book was translated into French under the title *Et Frappe A Mort Le Père,* my publishers gave a party to which they invited anyone in Paris who might be interested in the novel to attend, including Bill Coleman. He had lived in Paris since the early Thirties except for the War, and had always been an important figure in the French jazz scene. At this party he and I met for the first time and he has since become one of my greatest friends. I had written a portrait of my idea of what he must have been like before I knew him! I might now make a better job of the character if I were to write it after having known him ten years. A rambling answer but I hope with some point.

173

Your most recent novel, Winter In The Hills, *is an account of life in Wales, the result of your association with North Wales for the past fourteen years. You grasp the nettle of Welsh nationality firmly in the book, the question of two nations living in uneasy relationship, one, the Welsh, virtually occupied by the other, the English. You summarise this in a neat piece of symbolism, a bus service taking passengers up and down Caernarvon into the hills. Had this theme been building up in you for a long time?*

A writer's gifts are to some extent parasitic, like tendrils that reach out to whatever is going by. As a writer one processes one's experience into words in narrative or lyric form or dramatic form; the tendrils attach themselves accordingly to whatever is available. If I had married a Scotswoman and got deeply involved in Scotland then I would no doubt have written about Scotland, but in the event I married a Welshwoman which brought me deeply into contact with Welsh life, particularly as she was not an expatriate but someone deeply rooted in Wales. We have a little house here which we stay in very often and my wife is Welsh speaking, so we were soon in an enclave which English visitors will not expect to get into. After we first came here in 1960 it took me seven or eight years before I had the nerve to feel I knew enough about it to attempt a novel about it. I am not saying that everything I do is just for the sake of writing a book about it, but whatever aspect of life your experience brings you face to face with, that is where you do your work. It isn't that one says, 'Ha! That is good material!' but just that as life moves one around like a snooker ball across the table so one goes with it – I might have a son who worked on a North Sea oil rig and that might have been the subject of a novel – but one rolls in the direction one's pushed.

I think I might have had an interest in Wales anyway because, coming from North Staffordshire where the nearest sea coast is North Wales, I have always known the Wales of the holiday resorts, but suddenly at one stride I was into the Wales that really is Welsh and which for six hundred years has somehow resisted being processed into another region of England. It was chance again, but one goes where life dictates and wherever it is one looks for the reality and when that is seen that is what goes into the work.

Are you a methodical writer, nine to five? Could you answer that by describing a typical year in your life as a writer?

To start with a typical week. Like everyone else I have days off, perhaps Saturday and Sunday like an office worker, or perhaps midweek. On working days I work in the morning always, from nine till one, then again from about half past four until about seven. If I'm working full tilt on something like a novel and am in peak physical and mental condition, I might be able to work through those two sessions of the day for perhaps three days, after which I'm completely clapped out, and then I devote my working time to tidying my desk, answering letters, anything, but generally that is the pattern of a working week. I never work in the afternoon and never at night. Even when I was eighteen I formed the idea that the day was for work and the evening was for talking and drinking with one's friends or listening to records or just sitting around, so that if I'm working at night it means there is a crisis on, perhaps the last week of finishing a book, just as a student one worked if there was an essay crisis. On the other hand I get up early, so that my day is very like the day of most of the world's population. After dinner I settle the problems of the universe over a bottle of something. So I'm a five day a week writer and I try not to work more, though of course may have to go to London or accept an invitation to speak to a literary club and because that has to come out of my working time I am rather tough about accepting invitations to speak.

I write fiction and poetry and at the moment I'm writing a play*. Poetry is just something which really just has to come; you write a poem at twelve o'clock at night coming home in the train when the poem comes. On the other hand, a novel has a lot of earth-moving work; the great scene that has to be good can be skipped until you feel on top of the world, but ordinary scenes where the characters are being moved about or dialogue is being written – that is work and must be carried on, but the great moment when it has to be supremely good, you leave till later. That is why no one ever writes a novel from page one to page three hundred. What happens is that a start is made on page one, then gaps are left, and as in life, if you had control of it you would leave the great moments until you felt most yourself.

Do you think the novel has a future in the traditional sense? Or will the documentary fulfil its purpose?

After thinking about it for twenty five years, after mature reflection I cannot see that the invented story can be dispensed with. If civilisation

Harry In The Night, first produced 1975.

holds together in any form that we recognise and doesn't become Martian, if the present organisation of human life holds together at all, then there will be a place for the long, detailed account of events which have not actually taken place, because only the writer who is free to make up the action can fully convey his view of what the world is. The historian must wait for events, he can't write until the action has taken place, and he must be true to what actually happened, and what actually happened is so full of contradictions, full of coincidence, chance, whereas the novelist can say, 'This is what I think human beings are like. This is how I think they are going to act. This is my vision of life,' and he can weave his story in complete freedom. I don't see that we can ever do without it, though I know that in my own life I can go for months without ever opening a novel, but live on what's happening around me, people who come to tell me what happens to them or who ring me up at two o'clock in the morning to tell me they're desperate, that their marriage has broken up ...

This happens to you?

Yes – doesn't it happen to you and to everybody? Yet after months of that, I have to sit down with a novel and let somebody tell me a story which I know didn't literally happen but did happen because people are like that. Narrative has never had more of a hold than it has now. The power of narrative is such that if *The Forsyte Saga* appears on television, millions of people sit and watch it spellbound, longing for the next instalment, like children who have to be told a story. Why has the Archers lasted a quarter of a century? Because people must have a story. And I'm like that, though since I've been immersed a little more deeply in these things, the Archers won't quite do and the television adaptation of Galsworthy won't quite do, but never mind, when I sit down to *War And Peace* I know I am the same as all these who are breaking a leg to get to the television to see the next instalment.

The story imposes a kind of meaning on life, so I don't see any break in the power of the novel unless society becomes something unrecognisable. It may be that society moves into a state which has no use for narrative or linguistic expression at all, but in that case I couldn't take an interest in it any more than I could in what happens on Mars. The novel, the verbally conveyed imagined narrative, is as firmly part of what people want as food and drink.

Do you have any picture of your readers or do you simply write and – that's it, there will be readers? I take it that you hope something will happen to your readers as a result of reading your work other than having been merely diverted?

Oh, I'm a preacher. Good God, I'm not going to take all that trouble just to write books to amuse people. Of course I want the reader to share my values, but I realise it is no good simply telling him what those values are; one has to dramatise them. I am making up stories which express all my realities and I hope they will reach the reader at a deep level so that he won't even know when I'm preaching at him. I want him to accept the world I give him, to identify with the characters, share the emotions, and if he does that then I don't need to preach. I can't write a story that doesn't convey my reality and if the reader is moved by it that is better than any preaching. I'm acting as Philip Sidney defined it in *The Defense Of Poetry* and Aristotle in his *Poetics*: giving the reality of the writer to the reality of the reader, and enriching it.

On the question of my readers and how I see them: one isn't at all times thinking in the same way or at the same level. Sometimes I do think about my readers, just as sometimes I think about my sales or my income, but there is a white hot moment when one is creating and one is jammed up against the reality, trying to find words for these things and there is no room for thoughts about readers; between oneself and the work even a paper thin thought could not get in. At other times one stands back and considers what kind of person reads one's stuff. I imagine them to be people like myself, the professional middle class, people who have been through some form of training, had their minds trained, perhaps technicians, doctors, teachers, business people. I suppose the natural reader for my books is the person who has been introduced to the life of the mind, who has at some stage of life had to read books and think – people like that, who after all are numerous, possibly as many as ten million out of the population of fifty million. I suppose I am aiming my thoughts at those types, but anyone who can hear me, tune into the message, God knows, blessings on them! A typical diagram of my reader would be of someone who in his work uses his mind or her mind, because since women have got out from under the kitchen sink they are included more and more.

Two personalities in your life; firstly, Kingsley Amis – you knew him?

I was at Oxford with him, in the same college! An incredibly energetic and amusing person, the best raconteur, the best entertainer I've ever known; I've seen him in a pub surrounded by people begging him to stop, tears of laughter choking them. His funny stories were complete with all sorts of impressions and imitations, his audience reduced to pulp. I have never seen an entertainer who could entertain as he could. And he is a man I owe a great deal to: his zest for life and relish for the differences of character and of idiom are a tonic. A superb mimic, bringing in ten or a dozen characters all differentiated by their accents – I used to tell him he was turning away a big income by not turning professional, but as he has managed to make a big income by his writing, obviously he was right and I was wrong.

Under the humour is there a seriousness?

I think so, I think so ... but I'm not prepared to put a signature to it, simply because I'm not quite sure.

The other presence I referred to earlier is F.R. Leavis, the giant critic of the past fifty years. I think you said you had met him?

Being educated at Oxford, I was at a distance from Leavis. He symbolised for us everything that Cambridge meant, the high and dry intellect, the ascetic, excluding, rigorous mind. You see, it is not for nothing that the division existing between Oxford and Cambridge has grown up over the years; Oxford has always been much more rooted in life, in what was going on, much more traffic between Oxford and London. Oxford has always been more drawn into the life of the country, while Cambridge, out in the fens, far to the East, not on the way to anywhere, has always been austere, devoted to pure sciences, mathematics has always flourished there; they have always looked down on Oxford as a place corrupted. There's a seventeenth century quatrain which summed it up, about the King giving something to Cambridge because it lacked loyalty and something 'to that Right Royal Body' Oxford because they wanted learning.

Oxford has always been under suspicion of being too closely associated with the Establishment, with their own hotline to Westminster and part of government, corrupted by wealth and influence. Cambridge was pure, incorruptible. No one went to Cambridge unless they wanted the pure milk of the intellect, and all this produced Cambridge arrogance which is far worse than Oxford's involvement in the world. So at Cambridge literature studies consist mostly in throwing out, 'You mustn't read that,' but when you come to those that must be read, they must be read with intense concentration. I understood that Leavis was Cambridge; I was sent to his work and I read thoroughly *Scrutiny* and I could see what Oxford people found against Leavis, the high priestly arrogance I couldn't go along with because North Staffordshire doesn't go along with that. I was a democrat in a way that Leavis is not. I was pleased when Leavis took enough notice of me on one occasion when in a group somewhere or other. He must have hoisted in that I existed, because years later he was thundering against contemporary writers, particularly Amis, and someone said, 'And Wain, too.' Leavis paused and said, 'Ah, Wain is different. Wain's an educated man.' When I heard that Leavis had described me as an educated man I felt it hadn't all been in vain!

From 1973 to 1978 you are Oxford Professor of Poetry. Does this entail any published work, or is it chiefly lectures to students as you see fit, or is there a programme you have to follow?

I have been living in Oxford since 1963, and during that time a lot of young undergraduates have come to my house and read me their poems, talked about their problems, and so I've already done some of the work of a Professor of Poetry. Now, by a vote of Oxford MAs, I am supposed to be doing that officially. All I have to do by Statute is to lecture once a term – three times in the academic year – and I have to judge the Newdigate Prize; apart from that, all I have to do is breathe in and out. I shall continue to be encouraging and take an interest in the young poets in Oxford, read their work, tell them where I think they could improve their work, and be helpful in that way. There is no Statutory obligation to publish the lectures but everyone does so, and I intend to write a book called *Professing Poetry* in which I will publish the lectures and put them into a continuum of narrative about the whole experience of being such a professor. Nobody has done that. Every Professor of Poetry has published his lectures but nobody has dealt with the experience. It is a unique job and there is nothing else quite like it, not an academic post but more an *encouraging* post affiliated to the University as a working poet. If I wanted to stick to the letter of the law, I need never emerge from my house or speak to anybody, but in fact I like to know what young poets are writing and so we have open house and they come.

It *is* an interesting institution and Oxford can claim some credit, because while American universities have their Poet In Residence, a sort of retainer poet paid to be around, Oxford had that idea as early as 1712, so although Oxford is supposed to be the very symbol of reaction and privilege, it has some very good ideas.

One of your predecessors in the post was W.H. Auden. Perhaps you could offer your impressions of him?

Auden was a fascinating person, complex, someone who could not be caught in a few sentences. He would make his bargain with the settled state of society – he was not the radical he is often seen as, nor a revolutionary; he was not a man who thought it should all be overturned and cast into the fire. On the other hand, he was a man who believed in making his own area of freedom within that society. The world is set up in certain ways, with governments, churches, armies, universities, legislative bodies, and a revolutionary will say it should all be burned away to start again from the bare earth, and personally I have never believed that because I don't think it can be remade that way. Auden was like that; he went along with it: if a university invited him, he was prepared to talk to their students, teach or whatever was required, and so he was willing to return to Oxford as Professor of Poetry. But underneath the surface he was concerned to be free, to make his own life. For instance, take a simple example, the demands of social life which most of us give in to: if Auden was asked to dinner he turned up at six o'clock on the dot, not 5.59 or 6.01, and then he would have a specific number of martinis, then the dinner, and at 9.30 he went home, whoever was his host. His work routine meant that he woke early in the morning and he was not going to stay up late at night. For the three and a half hours he was of good value, giving out more ideas than the rest of the diners together, and then promptly he would go home. I respect that enormously since I would never have the guts to do it. If I'm invited out I turn up at the time expected and go home when they expect me to. Auden's practice I do respect!

Arnold Wesker (1966)

Arnold Wesker, what I'd really want to do is to hear you talking about your big project, Centre 42, something about its origins and how it is faring to date? I have with me your first annual report, for 1961/62. In it you say, "A strange hysteria descends upon the English personality, especially the intelligentsia, when projects involving art and the people are put into operation. There immediately springs to mind the image of patronising salvationists wanting to do good." Has this image faded since 1961 or is it still as powerful as ever?

I think it has faded since 1961, because of Centre 42 and the recent White Paper[1] and Jennie Lee's appointment to office in the Ministry of Education. It now seems OK to talk about culture, and I think indications of this are not only the fact that centres of one sort or another are being opened all over the country but also articles are appearing, one very good example by Milton Shulman in the *Evening Standard* recently insisted that we should cease to be ashamed of using a word like 'culture.' I have an article here, sent to me from America, in the *New Republic* by a man called Michael Straight quoting a report by the Rockefeller Foundation about the arts and a panel set up by the Foundation: "The panel is motivated by the conviction that the arts are not for the privileged few but for the many and that their place is not at the periphery of society but at the centre. They are not just a form of recreation but central to our well being and happiness." He goes on to say that this statement would have carried no weight ten years ago, and I think that is true. With Jennie Lee saying it and with Arts Council members saying it, suggests that while that hysteria still exists, there are other forces emerging, and I think Centre 42 is very much responsible for changing the climate.

You in a way got in ahead of the present official climate which is from the Left and is making the pace, has been making the pace since October 1964. Do you think the feeling that culture is OK is due to a sense of establishmentism in the air? Probably approving of progressive movements like yours?

No – it may turn out that way but I feel that suddenly everybody is terrified of 'leisure,' the big bogey man, and I'm a little worried that this is exploited. We began in the beginning by talking about increased leisure, but

[1] *A Policy For The Arts* (February 1965)

181

I'm dropping that now because if that is used too much, then the *raison d'être* for encouragement in the arts is wrong. I don't think it should be suggested to people that they should read books and go to concerts in order to fill in their bored time; I think they should go to books and music and theatre having discovered a need for it in themselves, a need which would have to be satisfied whether there was more leisure or not – a much more healthy approach. But the bogey man of leisure is one of the reasons that official bodies are beginning to be concerned, and that is true of almost everything in this country where the big advances have been made: the powers-that-be are terrified for practical reasons. Education was able to get under way because they realised they needed technicians to work their machines and it made it easier for those who felt they needed education for its own sake to help it come about. The same thing is going to happen with the arts. I think just as we educate people the wrong way, I'm afraid if attention isn't paid, that the arts are going to emerge with the wrong mantle.

Are the arts always going to be the prerogative of the few, the minority, or do you think you can transform the few into more?

I don't know – I certainly think you can transform the few into more, but whether that few plus the more makes that few still a minority, I don't know. Something I've always said is that you can't organise a civilisation on any other assumption but that everyone is capable, and if you organise in that way then there will be a true norm even if it's still a minority, because it's a truer minority than if you work it any other way.

What about the question of discipline though? The old classical school used to instil the child with the discipline of letters, of Latin and Greek, nowadays it seems to be English Literature with strict examination of the text, schools of rigorous criticism. Does there not have to be a core of disciplinary attention to some subject or other in order to tap the capacity of most people and bring it out and so make them able and willing to expose themselves to the arts?

I think discipline is necessary but – it's a cliché – self-imposed discipline which comes about when one discovers one's own needs and desires, oneself. One of the things about Centre 42 is that we plan to have a special department that will have a close association with local educational establishments, subsidiary to the work of arts masters and mistresses, providing our own professional musicians, actors, directors and writers as lecturers in the arts so that they will be backed up by a whole cultural machinery; so that a playwright who takes on a course in a local school is able to take half a dozen actors from Centre 42 and so make more real the fact that our Centre will be open to the school. Remembering that we are only concerned with one Centre but that there must be other centres, as these centres grow and strike up an association with schools there will be a completely different approach to the subject of the arts in schools. I hope in this way it will take a more important place in the curriculum.

Are you wired into adult education in the same way? Would you want to be?

It's not that we would want to be – I don't *not* want to be – but it's just that they haven't been part of our consideration as yet.

They are really a previous generation, aren't they? The Keir Hardie generation of self-help. They haven't quite expired but there's something tired about them for a new Centre such as yours.

No, I don't think that was necessarily why I said that, but is a matter of planning ahead with what one imagines will be scarce resources. We just won't be able to cope with more than a limited area.

Can I ask what has happened since the first six provincial festivals – have you been continuing?

Nothing. There were one or two isolated events in the successful towns which were a little aborted because, though the intention was to keep the spirit alive, it cost too much money for the returns, so I made the decision that we would do absolutely nothing until we had a base and resources from which to operate. So we have concentrated only on raising money and getting the Roundhouse in London for the Centre, which we now have. That is the building and we're now raising the money to convert it. The only people who are at work are the architects.

But you're keeping contact with all the organisation, well-wishers and supporters who were behind you?

So far as they keep contact with us, but not otherwise; we don't publish a Newsletter though this is something that we might get to do as it becomes obvious that there's more to report.

Does this mean getting out and about in the provinces or do you do most of the work centrally from here?

It will mean someone getting out and about in the provinces –

As Clive Barker did originally –

This will be another important department of 42; not one person but a handful, as many as we can afford who will be responsible for audience contact, and that doesn't mean just audience contact in the local area but far afield. Ideally I want us to be so well organised and in touch with the provinces, that they are booked up with Centre 42 events many months in advance.

I enjoyed the Nottingham event so much that I was astonished to read that it was the least successful of the six places where the initial events took place, presumably because few were attracted to the programme? I do remember there were very few in the audience for Bernard Kops' play. I counted them - just 17!

That was poor local organisation because we had relied in all the six towns on the inviting committee undertaking the responsibility *ad hoc,* that is, it was their festival to which we were being invited but they had to go out and find the audience, and in Nottingham they didn't; they hadn't realised what they had taken on and so hadn't taken it that seriously.

In the future you will be making this new Centre at the Roundhouse your priority? Does it look like coming into effect in a year, two years?

Two years at the earliest.

May I finally ask you about your own work? Are you managing to find time for the writing of plays?

Two new plays are completed and waiting to go into production at the end of the year.[2]

So you are a creative artist and administrator in parallel? You can do both?

I don't know whether I can do both, since neither the new Centre 42 nor the new plays have yet been successful!

That must mean a lot of energy – it's not long since Chips With Everything, *is it?*

Oh, it's ages – about two and a half years.

[2] *The Four Seasons* and *Their Very Own And Golden City*

Are you able to say to yourself, "I will not write a play for another year," as I think you did originally decide?

No, I'm making no such drastic decisions. It so happens I haven't a play to write but I leave myself open whereas before I mentally blocked myself so as to devote time to creating Centre 42.

So when the spirit enters now the pen will move?

Something like that.

Note: The Centre 42 organisation was dissolved in 1970.

Angus Wilson (1976)

Before discussing your work, perhaps we could talk a little about your career in libraries. You spent the years from 1936 to 1955 in the British Museum Library, apart from war service, and I wonder if you could describe the environment of that institution, its atmosphere in those days?

I will try. When I left Oxford in the full Depression it was not easy even for graduates to get employment. I came down with a Second in History, probably through spending far too much time acting in the OUDS, and for the first year did odd jobs. Then I heard through Arthur Ellis who was Superintendent of the Reading Room, a well-known figure in the library world and one who enjoyed close relations with many of the old readers of the Reading Room. Through a friend of his I heard that there were vacancies on the staff of the Library because of a massive revision of the old 1840s catalogue which badly needed editing and publishing along modern lines. The British Museum persuaded the Treasury that if twenty people could be employed who were qualified in Latin and Greek, with French and German and possibly one other language, then the catalogue of the Library could be complete in about fifteen years, an up-to-date register of six million books. I had those qualifications, and even added Norwegian after I started working there. About sixteen or so of the new assistants had already begun when I arrived, including G.D. Painter, an expert on incunabula and author of a book on Proust, and Howard Nixon, the authority on bookbindings and now in charge of the muniments at Westminster Abbey.

Fifteen years? When I left in 1955 this mighty work had reached the letter D. I think this was because the estimate made by the scholarly gentlemen in the first place was all too 19th century, and that the art of cataloguing had moved on since then and was much more exacting. Later still, as you know, the publication was achieved in a much shorter space of time by the application of modern photostatting in the 1970s. Still, those earlier volumes were marvellous examples of cataloguing, done with scrupulous care. We were also expected to catalogue the new accessions as they came in, and in fact that was what I spent most of my time on until 1939. Just before the War, I was engaged on the cataloguing of a great find of French Revolutionary documents and that took me until I was called up for work in Intelligence.

What was the Museum like in those days?

We were paid, rather badly paid, by H.M. Treasury, and were not permanent but temporary civil servants and were indeed the servants of the Trustees, the august body of eminent men like the Archbishop of Canterbury and others in public life, together with representatives of the families of those who had made the great initial bequests to the Library, Cotton for instance; that has all gone now. Some of my colleagues had been on the staff since before the First World War and had worked under people like Sir Edmund Gosse, and Sir Richard Garnett and Sir Frederick Kenyon the Biblical scholar, so the atmosphere was curiously Victorian. One of the senior members of staff I can remember, who was concerned with the recataloguing of the stock under the complex heading 'Bible,' and his colleague who was responsible for classifying – these two gentlemen occupied a great deal of their leisure time, and I fear somewhat of their official time, producing Greek Alcaic poems about the cat in the Museum restaurant. This was the tail end of the Victorian age. At the lower end of the scale were the temporary clerks and the fetchers and carriers of the books who received poor wages and would enhance their wages by acting as butler or footmen at the banquets held for the Trustees. This still continued into the 1930s, after such a banquet finding the older library attendants in the stacks below the Reading Room, amidst all that ironwork, somnolent after sharing some of the perks they had enjoyed, half a partridge and half a bottle of champagne. The whole place was like a Dickens world. I never regretted having seen it. Under the Copyright Act we received everything; I believe we could only refuse things which gave prices and betting odds of horses. I learned a great deal about the publishing trade, for instance the vast mass of romantic novels and of religious publishing which I knew nothing about and provincial publications from a huge number of presses. We were untrained in the modern sense and the British Museum Catalogue was constructed on its own rules which had been worked out in Maunde Thompson's day in the 1860s.

The books were brought to us on barrows by ex-Service men who wore their medals, and I would feel bewildered when I saw books in a language quite strange to me, in one case they turned out to be Welsh and I was expected to tackle them with the aid of a Welsh-English dictionary; the same went for Danish and Dutch – 'You can work it out from the languages you know' – that was the attitude. When I returned from the War, I was given an interesting job: 300,000 books were lost in the bombing, and I had the task of trying to replace them; in four years I replaced a quarter of them through attending sales and auctions and visiting private houses and advertising. We had the pick of the books which had been sent for salvage and which were thought to contain some valuable stuff. One I remember was a Hebrew MS dating back to Queen Elizabeth's reign thrown out by a canon's wife in a patriotic mood during the War.

The old Victorian atmosphere persisted. I recall an old Keeper who dated from the 1900 period saying to me, "One thing you must be very proud of is that you are working in George III's Library, unique in the world" – then I came to work one morning to see the Keeper in a helmet and gumboots wading about in the mud and debris. I said what a tragedy that the King's Library should have been destroyed, and he said, "My dear boy, there wasn't anything in it which wouldn't have been in any gentleman's library."

From the date of my job replacing the lost books, about 1950, until I left in 1955, I had what was the most satisfying post and my happiest years, as Assistant to the Superintendent of the Reading Room, first to Rendell, then to Robert Wilson, then to Noel Clarke. I believe that, had I been in the Reading Room before I started to write as a hobby, I would never have started to write. The job was absorbing, I loved being with the readers. Yesterday at the Royal Society of Literature, I was introducing a speaker and in the audience were a number of people who remembered me in the Reading Room, and I'm always pleased when people come up and say I'd been helpful. Undertaking research for people, individual pieces of work, had some totality, unlike continuous cataloguing which was so fluid. To be perfectly honest, I was a good librarian when dealing with people and their queries and so with the contents of books, but not a good librarian when I was working on incunabula and had changed the month of the year of publication because in the earliest books the month as well as the year was printed, and I had read the long Franciscan sermon from which I deduced that the book could not have been printed in the month given in the imprint. The senior cataloguer said, 'Oh, we don't read these things, we go by the date as printed.' But that was not my way, I fear; I liked the public side of the work at the Museum, and to some extent my novel, *The Old Men At The Zoo,* is a

189

satire about the workings of the Museum. The different approaches to the running of the Zoo are parallel to the different approaches to the running of the Museum. My intention in that book was to make it an imaginary picture of the Zoo, which was symbolic of England, in the event of a Nazi takeover. But I was told that it would be a matter of libel if I made the Keeper of Reptiles a Nazi sympathiser, since when I got to know the Keepers who told me that was nonsense, nevertheless I laid it in the future and an imaginary war. Still, the attitudes I described were all based on the officials at the British Museum when I was there, and their views of the public.

Did the literature that you handled in such quantities feed your imagination, get you started as a novelist?

No. I wouldn't say that was so. My writing comes out of my boyhood and the reading of fiction. I don't know that the Library affected my writing except in that one instance. I don't think I was cut out to be a librarian, although I think I would have been happy to go on working in the public departments. I feel very happy whenever I visit the Reading Room and I will be sad if it should ever disappear in my lifetime because it was a wonderful place to work in and with some extraordinary people as readers. Often I was in sole charge for months at a time, and then I used to say that my job was somewhere between a learned person and a vicar, encouraging and asking how their work was going. And there were some very curious people who came in from time to time; once I was asked to go out and speak to a man lighting matches and throwing them around the room. I approached him, a big man, an Austrian, and said I was sorry but he couldn't light matches in the Reading Room, and he upped and felled me to the ground. Other readers came up to say how brave I had been but I hadn't been brave at all. I had just stood there and been felled to the ground!

That is a world that has passed, to be replaced by utilitarian students filling the desks in most large reference libraries.

Yes, there were then so many characters of private means. The Superintendent I mentioned, Arthur Ellis, was outraged when it was suggested that there might have to be a reduction in the readers admitted because of the danger of glass from the great dome when the bombs fell; they would be confined to the North Library. He was furious because one lady was considered for exclusion on the grounds that her work was not all that important. He said, "It's damnable! We can't possibly take her ticket away from her – look what she's doing for the war effort: she's putting her Gaelic on one side and translating Virgil into French." It was a home for lame ducks in those days, it must be said.

If I can pass to your work as a writer now. How does a novelist see? Tangibly, literally, metamorphically, when he starts on a novel? When you sit down do you begin with a situation or a character or is there some deeper sense in which you see the structure of the object you are going to make, before you begin?

I would say that in nearly all cases they begin with a momentary vision. In the one novel recently made into a four-part television series, *Late Call,* about a hotel manageress retiring and having to find her life again with her son who is headmaster of a school in a new town, I began with a fleeting glimpse of a woman whom I had seen standing by a gate looking over a stretch of flat countryside in Suffolk. She was dressed like a townee, a middle aged, stoutish woman looking sad, very much not a country woman, but urban and dressy. That was what set the whole tale going.

Again, I was at the Museum when the Sutton Hoo burial was found and I was often having tea in the canteen with colleagues. Now at that early state, the interpretation was accepted fully, simply on the reputation of the principal archaeologist, and it occurred to me that if someone chose to play a perverse joke on the archaeologists, taking advantage of their honesty, then an interesting contretemps could result. Just before that discovery there had been the Piltdown hoax, which combined with that notion of mine, I could see how the two things went together to suggest a theme: how easily, from vanity, a specialist would not relinquish a theory once committed to it, or out of loyalty to an authority now dead who had first propounded the theory, and they feel unwilling to question it. Now that kind of idea will work in my mind for a time.

It's a long process. I write in longhand in exercise books for I've never learned to type and in typing I wouldn't feel I was in control. I leave the opposite page empty, to add additions and corrections later.

And you write more fluently that way?

Yes; another reason I don't type is because I revise immediately as I write and correct as I go along. I write regularly from nine till about four now that

I'm getting older – in the old days I would stop at five. I like to write out of doors and go abroad where it is hot in winter, though I haven't managed it with the present book, on Kipling*, because all the notes are here. Writing a novel, I will go out into a banana plantation or to Morocco, which is something I am able to do now, but when I left the British Museum I had no pension and only £300 in the world. I thought I would take advantage of the freedom to live in the country with a garden and then to travel which I've been able to do extensively for the last twenty years, usually in the winter with my secretary who drives me out into the desert, with some oranges, and time passes quickly until four o'clock when he fetches me again. I need complete quiet; even out in the desert I will use earplugs.

If I use, say six or seven exercise books to a novel, there will also be six or seven exercise books about the characters, preparatory. I can take a very long time thinking myself into the story, and all of it goes on to paper. I start with a little bit of business – in *Late Call*, for example, I know the hotel world well and so make my main character a hotel manageress, and then introduce a mother and father who resemble the parents of a friend of mine and like my own parents. I write dialogues between them. Then I had an idea of childhood, and looked for some books about childhood and farm life in 1911 including the weather; the result is the scene set in 1911. After that I will make a family tree so that I am sure what age such-and-such a character would be in 1936, if twelve in 1911. I think the vision I have of people comes from my training as a geographical historian, so that I see people in time terms like a genealogical tree, with the dates like a date map, and then in geographical terms. Hence, now I see Harold at 36 but remember that he was twelve, and at twelve he was down in Sussex and at 36 he is up in Herefordshire.

That was important in No Laughing Matter.

Enormously important. And just as important in *As If By Magic* with them all moving about across Asia and while Henry is in one place and Alexandra in another, and while writing the Henry scenes and Alexandra scenes, I was all the time conscious that they were going to meet in Goa and that they would die there. And it was similar in *Anglo Saxon Attitudes*, reverting to Gerald's past, and in *Hemlock And After* I worked out the scene in Vardon Hall, the founding of the Hall, which I realised

*The Strange Ride Of Rudyard Kipling (1977)

only when I had finished it, that it was based on a village I had lived in during the War, in Hertfordshire. Then I had to unmake much of it because the woman who was the basis for Mrs Currie lived near there and, although she is now dead, I couldn't have let that appear in the novel, hence I rewrote one scene in St Albans, which made nonsense of it in a way.

So it is a lengthy process: if I spend, as I do, about eighteen months on a novel, one year or even a little more is spent planning it. I do a lot of revision when I have finished, in addition to the daily revisions, and the last page I write so furiously that I just have to leave notes to return to and rewrite when I'm not so tired.

What about the emotions as you write?

They flame! I usually feel very exhausted and have to watch that I take holidays now and again, because as a freelance the danger is not to take notice of the time. When abroad I will write for two weeks in one place, then we motor somewhere else and the three or four days motoring are a compulsory holiday, relaxing; being driven I find very relaxing. That is the way I write. Dialogue is extremely important to me, I must be able to establish a *voice* for my characters before I see what happens, and also an *internal* voice and I am more and more concerned with place. It is very important, even in a small paragraph, to feel that I have established place. That's what appeals to me in Kipling's writing – his incredible sense of place.

It has struck me in reading your novels that you see people as performers and society as a kind of theatre with a hint of the counterfeit that you are trying to probe or even to mock?

Yes, this is true, and I'm also trying to find out what is the real, interior theatre. Are they still playing parts even when they are speaking to themselves or is there a reality beneath? Yes, stripping off layers is essential to me. My own family were histrionic and given to play-acting, especially when going down in the world socially and financially, when they would be extremely lively and vivacious, the more to conceal their own panic from themselves, and perhaps all my novels have this quality of revelation: *The Middle Age Of Mrs Eliot* discloses that her husband didn't love her as much as she thought, and she thought she was a smart society hostess who could do anything she liked, which wasn't true. Gerald in *Anglo Saxon*

Attitudes having to discover what is his relationship to his family and to scholarship, and Bernard in *Hemlock* what are his attitudes towards the young? Simon Carter in *Anglo Saxon Attitudes* – can one be a scientist and administrator at the same time?

I suppose it all comes from the motivation in my own case. I began writing when I was at the Museum and had had a nerve-racked childhood, doting parents and elder brothers, divorce and other melodramas; my mother died when I was fifteen, my father when I was older. Not an unhappy childhood, but churned up. After that, the War, isolated doing Intelligence work in the country and when I came back to the Museum it was to continue the cataloguing work, not very rewarding. I had been active in Labour Party politics and now in 1945 the Labour Party had come to power and I felt no great need to carry on with that; amateur acting which had been my hobby seemed drearier as one got older. Hence I think I was forced to look into myself, and that came about by sitting down one Sunday and starting to write. That was a story called 'Raspberry Jam,' the first of twelve stories which made up into *The Wrong Set,* and their first appearance was odd: a painter whom I knew had been staying at the weekend and the next thing I knew was a telephone call from Cyril Connolly at *Horizon.* The painter had shown him the stories and Connolly said he wanted to publish them in *Horizon.* I didn't even know anyone had an inkling I'd written the stories. They seemed to be liked, and a friend at Secker & Warburg – still my publishers – said that if I had more, to make up twelve, they might make a book. I replied that I had twelve, and so the book came out.

I had no plan to become a professional writer and kept telling myself that I wasn't, that it would be a part-time occupation, until it became apparent that my two occupations were not compatible, especially when I was writing a play and dealing with management and rehearsals, so I was forced to make a decision and I think it was the right one – but it *was* difficult. I did like the Reading Room very much.

How about your novels as judgement? Are you judging as you write?

I try not to be too much of a judge of morals but I'm basically rather a Puritan; my father, although a professional gambler, must have come from Presbyterian stock and my mother was brought up a Congregationalist. I suppose there is a strong moral balance in them, less so in my later works where I think there is more playing around with words, experimenting, plays within a play in *No Laughing Matter*. With some success in writing and the possibility of occupying a very minor place in textbooks, I'm aware of the ancestry of novels, and so take care. In my first novel there was a character called Ron, an unsuccessful little crook, and I wrote that when he went to prison he had a success that he had never had during this novel. An American publisher said this must be a mistake since it wasn't done to mention the novel when writing the same novel; it destroys the realism. But that has always been in me, to remind people that it is a novel – part of the Fielding tradition of realism.

Now that you are a Professor at East Anglia lecturing on English Literature, does this double persona conflict with your writing – you are now both an analytical critic and a creative writer?

You are absolutely right to ask that because it's the one aspect I am worried about. I do teach rather seldom, only once a week and only in the summer terms so it is very much part-time, but it is worrying and I've said until I retire in four years' time I won't do any more teaching in America; I may take that on then if I need the money. But I do think that too much academic work does make one over-critical and over literary-conscious. On the other hand, one is confronted with this issue that while periodically my books do well and I needn't think about making money, this is not always so and certainly wasn't so when I started writing, and one wonders what other things one can do which do the least harm to the writing and which occupies the least time while earning enough money to cope. I enjoy teaching and I enjoy reviewing and that I do easily, but it is increasingly worrying about criticising other peoples' work and I won't review novels now because I know how difficult it is to write one and I'm not going into print criticising brother and sister novelists. And much energy can be wasted that way – Cyril Connolly ended up not writing what he could have done because he was editing and writing reviews. Is it better to write reviews? Is it better to do lecturing? Some friends have gone into television attracted by the money they can get and so leave writing altogether, so it is something that needs deciding, and I decided that the least harmful and the most enjoyable was lecturing, which was valuable because it brought me into touch with younger people.

To finish on a bread and butter note – relations with publishers. Has your relationship with publishers always been good?

Yes, I think so. I have always had an agent, and that I believe is a wise move because if a writer doesn't know publishers at the outset or isn't a good businessman, as I am not, then it's useful to have a professional bargainer. If you do know the publisher it is embarrassing to feel that they may not be treating you as well as they should because they are friends. So an agent obviates all that, and in the beginning he can get all sorts of work and foreign translations later which on your own you couldn't get. Perhaps later it is possible to work out contracts without help, especially with publishers known to you, but even then it is always possible to manage better terms through an agent – and I have been with the same publisher throughout.

As to social relations with publishers, I know my publishers well but I don't see them a great deal, and I'm not interested in publishing per se but on a personal basis I like to talk about books to my English publisher and I know my French publisher very well. I'm not one to spend much time in the publishing world or indeed with the literary world; I know most writers and have a few very good friends among them and I like to think I can be of help to younger writers. I believe I've done my stint for the literary cause, on the Royal Society of Literature committee and as Chairman of the Arts Council Literature Panel for three years – a hard job. I was also Chairman of the National Book League, and I was involved in demonstrations over Public Lending Right. I'm political at heart and such involvements I thought right. Literary parties I do *not* go to and I won't have them for my own books – I don't like the atmosphere. If we have a success with a book then we can have a party after its success, but the parties on launching a book to which the critics come I don't like. I don't want to be present sharing a drink with a critic while he's being cordial and knowing that he is thinking up something nasty to say about the new novel.

I am always keyed up about what happens to my books and find it hard to cope with bad notices and reviews, and that is bad enough without adding to it at literary parties. I will give interviews to help promote the book because it helps the publisher, but not to hobnob with critics over cocktails. So on the whole my relations with publishers have always been easy; I've never quitted a publisher and have always thought it wise not to do. Other writers have said, 'Why don't you go to So-and-So for a change?' and perhaps I might have done better on occasion but it is better to remain, and indeed often writers tell me they did no better with a new publisher. One other factor is availability: one reason why it is impossible to get hold of H.G. Well's novels now is because he went to about twenty different publishers after quarrelling with many of them, so that no publisher finds it worthwhile to keep his books in print because no publisher controls them all. It is better to settle with one publisher early on, then when he is still your publisher later you are in a better position.